Pagan Portals
&
Shaman Pathways

...an ever-growing library of shared knowledge.

Moon Books has created two unique series where leading authors
and practitioners come together to share their knowledge,
passion and expertise across the complete Pagan spectrum. If you
would like to contribute to either series, our proposal procedure
is simple and quick, just visit our website (www.MoonBooks.net)
and click on Author Inquiry to begin the process.

If you are a reader with a comment about a book or a suggestion
for a title we'd love to hear from you! You can find us at
facebook.com/MoonBooks or you can keep up to date with new
releases etc on our dedicated Portals page at facebook.com/
paganportalsandshamanpathways/

*'Moon Books has achieved that rare feat of being synonymous with top-
quality authorship AND being endlessly innovative and exciting.'*
Kate Large, Pagan Dawn

T0159068

Pagan Portals

Animal Magic, Rachel Patterson
An introduction to the world of animal magic and working with animal spirit guides

Australian Druidry, Julie Brett
Connect with the magic of the southern land, its seasons, animals, plants and spirits

Blacksmith Gods, Pete Jennings
Exploring dark folk tales and customs alongside the magic and myths of the blacksmith Gods through time and place

Brigid, Morgan Daimler
Meeting the Celtic Goddess of Poetry, Forge, and Healing Well

By Spellbook & Candle, Mélusine Draco
Why go to the bother of cursing, when a bottling or binding can be just as effective?

By Wolfsbane & Mandrake Root, Mélusine Draco
A study of poisonous plants, many of which have beneficial uses in both domestic medicine and magic

Candle Magic, Lucya Starza
Using candles in simple spells, seasonal rituals and essential craft techniques

Celtic Witchcraft, Mabh Savage
Wield winds of wyrd, dive into pools of wisdom; walk side by side with the Tuatha Dé Danann

Dancing with Nemetona, Joanna van der Hoeven
An in-depth look at a little-known Goddess who can help bring
peace and sanctuary into your life

Fairy Witchcraft, Morgan Daimler
A guidebook for those seeking a path that combines modern
Neopagan witchcraft with the older Celtic Fairy Faith

God-Speaking, Judith O'Grady
What can we do to save the planet? Three Rs are not enough.
Reduce, reuse, recycle...and religion

Gods and Goddesses of Ireland,
Meet the Gods and Goddesses of Pagan Ireland in myth and
modern practice

Grimalkyn: The Witch's Cat, Martha Gray
A mystical insight into the cat as a power animal

Hedge Riding, Harmonia Saille
The hedge is the symbolic boundary between the two worlds and
this book will teach you how to cross that hedge

Hedge Witchcraft, Harmonia Saille
Learning by experiencing is about trusting your instincts and
connecting with your inner spirit

Hekate, Vivienne Moss
The Goddess of Witches, Queen of Shades and Shadows, and
the ever-eternal Dark Muse haunts the pages of this poetic
devotional, enchanting those who love Her with the charm only
this Dark Goddess can bring

Herbs of the Sun, Moon and Planets, Steve Andrews
The planets that rule over herbs that grow on Earth

Hoodoo, Rachel Patterson
Learn about and experience the fascinating magical art of
Hoodoo

Irish Paganism, Morgan Daimler
Reconstructing the beliefs and practices of pre-Christian Irish
Paganism for the modern world

Kitchen Witchcraft, Rachel Patterson
Take a glimpse at the workings of a Kitchen Witch and share in
the crafts

Meditation, Rachel Patterson
An introduction to the beautiful world of meditation

Merlin: Once and Future Wizard, Elen Sentier
Merlin in history, Merlin in mythology, Merlin through the ages
and his continuing relevance

Moon Magic, Rachel Patterson
An introduction to working with the phases of the Moon

Nature Mystics, Rebecca Beattie
Tracing the literary origins of modern Paganism

Pan, Mélusine Draco
An historical, mythological and magical insight into the God Pan

Pathworking through Poetry, Fiona Tinker
Discover the esoteric knowledge in the works of Yeats, O'Sullivan
and other poets

Runes, Kylie Holmes

The Runes are a set of 24 symbols that are steeped in history, myths and legends. This book offers practical and accessible information for anyone to understand this ancient form of divination

Sacred Sex and Magick, Web PATH Center

Wrap up ecstasy in love to create powerful magick, spells and healing

Spirituality without Structure, Nimue Brown

The only meaningful spiritual journey is the one you consciously undertake

The Awen Alone, Joanna van der Hoeven

An introductory guide for the solitary Druid

The Cailleach, Rachel Patterson

Goddess of the ancestors, wisdom that comes with age, the weather, time, shape-shifting and winter

The Morrigan, Morgan Daimler

On shadowed wings and in raven's call, meet the ancient Irish Goddess of war, battle, prophecy, death, sovereignty, and magic

Urban Ovate, Brendan Howlin

Simple, accessible techniques to bring Druidry to the wider public

Your Faery Magic, Halo Quin

Tap into your Natural Magic and become the Fey you are

Zen Druidry, Joanna van der Hoeven
Zen teachings and Druidry combine to create a peaceful life path
that is completely dedicated to the here and now

Shaman Pathways

Aubry's Dog, Melusine Draco
A practical and essential guide to using canine magical energies

Black Horse White Horse, Mélusine Draco
Feel the power and freedom as Black Horse, White Horse guides
you down the magical path of this most noble animal

Celtic Chakras, Elen Sentier
Tread the British native shaman's path, explore the Goddess
hidden in the ancient stories; walk the Celtic chakra spiral
labyrinth

Druid Shaman, Danu Forest
A practical guide to Celtic shamanism with exercises and
techniques as well as traditional lore for exploring the Celtic
Otherworld

Elen of the Ways, Elen Sentier
British shamanism has largely been forgotten: the reindeer
Goddess of the ancient Boreal forest is shrouded in mystery...
follow her deer-trods to rediscover her old ways

Following the Deer Trods, Elen Sentier
A practical handbook for anyone wanting to begin the old British
paths. Follows on from Elen of the Ways

Trees of the Goddess, Elen Sentier
Work with the trees of the Goddess and the old ways of Britain

Way of the Faery Shaman, Flavia Kate Peters
Your practical insight into Faeries and the elements they engage
to unlock real magic that is waiting to help you

Web of Life, Yvonne Ryves
A new approach to using ancient ways in these contemporary
and often challenging times to weave your life path

What people are saying about

The Hedge Druid's Craft

Liminal places hold great power and deep magic; they are spaces between worlds, between times, and between states of being. Learning how to cross these boundaries brings insight, wisdom, and transformation. *The Hedge Druid's Craft* by Joanna Van Der Hoeven presents a unique approach to spiritual practice which straddles the worlds between Witchcraft and Druidry, and lays out a clear pathway for those who seek to learn how to ride the hedge in their own work. While the book is filled with practical information, accessible tools, and inspired workings, it is van der Hoeven's beautifully written sharings of her personal experiences and Otherworldly encounters which makes *The Hedge Druid's Craft* truly shine. **Jhenah Telyndru**, founder of the Sisterhood of Avalon and author of *Avalon Within, The Avalonian Oracle*, and *Rhiannon: Divine Queen of the Celtic Britons*

What a wonderful book! Written with real warmth and clarity, Joanna van der Hoeven explores the diverse practices of the hedge druid and its sister paths of Witchcraft Wicca and Druidry. Genuine, grounded and packed full of useful knowledge and techniques this book is a real find. Whilst sharing her personal experiences and insights Jo shows you all you need to work with ancestors and faeries, the world tree, animals and herbs and so much more to add a touch of the wild to your own practice and help you dive through the hedge and explore this path for yourself. A perfect introduction for the 21st century hedge rider. **Danu Forest**, author of *The Druid Shaman, The Magical Year, Celtic Tree Magic* and more.

The Hedge Druid is a liminal figure, walking along the borders, spanning the realms of the formally-trained Druid and the self-taught cunning woman (or man). Joanna van der Hoeven brings us powerful inspiration for breaking down the boundaries in our own lives and letting magic seep into every corner. Packed full of rituals and lore to guide the reader on their own journey across the hedge, *The Hedge Druid's Craft* offers a bounty of ideas for Pagans of many paths to re-enchant their lives."

Laura Perry, author of *Ariadne's Thread: Awakening the Wonders of the Ancient Minoans in our Modern Lives, The Minoan Tarot & Ancient Spellcraft: From the Hymns of the Hittites to the Carvings of the Celts*

Pagan Portals

The Hedge Druid's Craft

An Introduction to Walking Between the Worlds
of Wicca, Witchcraft and Druidry

Pagan Portals

The Hedge Druid's Craft

An Introduction to Walking Between the Worlds
of Wicca, Witchcraft and Druidry

Joanna van der Hoeven

MOON
BOOKS

Winchester, UK
Washington, USA

First published by Moon Books, 2018
Moon Books is an imprint of John Hunt Publishing Ltd., No. 3 East Street, Alresford
Hampshire SO24 9EE, UK
office1@jhpbooks.net
www.johnhuntpublishing.com
www.moon-books.net

For distributor details and how to order please visit the 'Ordering' section on our website.

Text copyright: Joanna van der Hoeven 2017

ISBN: 978 1 78535 796 1
978 1 78535 797 8 (ebook)
Library of Congress Control Number: 2017947283

A CIP catalogue record for this book is available from the British Library.

Design: Stuart Davies

Printed and bound by CPI Group (UK) Ltd, Croydon, CR0 4YY, UK

We operate a distinctive and ethical publishing philosophy in
all areas of our business, from our global network of authors to
production and worldwide distribution.

Contents

Acknowledgements

In deepest gratitude the Fair Folk and the spirits of place. I honour you for all that you are, with all that I am.

Introduction from the author

I have always been a Witch.

I have not always been a Druid.

I practice a mostly solitary form of Western Paganism, in which I would call myself a Hedge Druid and a Witch. Explaining this to others in everyday life would require a long and lengthy explanation, however, and so I normally simply state that I am a Druid. For me, the Hedge Druid is one who blends the natural lore and folk customs of the local area, alongside the teachings and mythology of the Celtic Druids to create his or her own path. In my own work, it's a blend of what is often called Witchcraft, Wicca and Druidry: The Hedge Druid's Craft.

For me, being a Witch is a natural thing, something that you are born with. It's a talent, an ability, much like being musically or artistically proficient. That's not to say that people can't learn, but most Witches that I know, myself included, have always lived their lives a little differently, a little on the edge from the mainstream. It's finding the magic and enchantment in everyday life. It's about encounters with the Fair Folk. It's about walking between the worlds. It's about intuitively being able to communicate with animals, plants, or people on a deeper level than most are able to achieve.

Being a Druid is somewhat more akin to training, rather than intuition. The Classical writers have informed us that historically, the Druids took around nineteen years of study before they could claim the title of Druid. Now, I'm not saying that you have to study for nineteen years before you can call yourself a Druid today, though some Druids would disagree with me. It was said that those from the continent sent their best and brightest to the British Isles to train in Druid studies, which included mathematics, geography, language, biology, the arts and more. There is a sort of similarity between these studies and our own public education

1

system. We get around 12 years of basic education, with a further 5-6 years of higher education on top of that, should we choose/are able to do so. So, that totals around 17-18 years of an education, at any rate. This forms a large part of our secular studying, in coming to learn more about the world wherein we live. But for the Druid it doesn't stop there. We also immerse ourselves in the history and mythology of the Celts, of locality and the environment, and what we know of the Druids themselves, both ancient and modern. That helps us to round out our Druid training.

I studied Wicca when I first delved into Pagan studies. Wicca is the modern formal religion which is supposed to have derived from or at least inspired by the older form of Witchcraft. I was around eighteen or nineteen years old, and began performing solitary rituals, casting spells and dancing under the light of the full moon and honouring deity in a male and female form. I came to Druidry later in life, when I was in my thirties. At first, it seemed too dry and staid, and so I left Druidry behind and studied Buddhism and Zen for a few years. Then Druidry called me back. Through the teachings of a very wise (and wild) woman I found a strand of Druidry that spoke to my soul, of hiking deep into the forest and meeting the ancestors, feeling the draw and magnetic pull of the new moon, honouring the tides and times of life and questing the awen, or inspiration.

The three paths met, and have blended together for me in my own personal work. Externally, I have always simply called myself a Druid, and presented Druidry as I have learned it through my many teachers and research, study and practice. But internally, I have always honoured the wild witch inside, the one who can shape and change her fate, who knows where the badgers live, who talks to the crows flying overhead on their way home to their roosts, who casts spells by the seashore. I also honour my former Wiccan work and practice, which I found at a very crucial point in my life and which helped me to become the person I am today. This work is an expression of a very deep part of my life, and my soul, which I now share with you.

So, for me (and for the purposes of this book) the Hedge Druid's Craft is for one who is intuitively a Witch, and who has also trained and studied as a Druid and a Wiccan. This differs from the common perception of a Hedge Druid, which is simply a solitary Druid, much as one would equate a Hedge Witch in a similar vein. This stems from the nineteenth-century term, "hedge priest", which denoted a priest who was not dedicated or affiliated with a particular church, and who preached "from the hedgerow". In the twentieth century, the term Hedge Witch was developed to denote a solitary witch, who was not affiliated to any particular tradition or coven. The author Rae Beth made the term "Hedge Witch" popular in the 1990s, and it is her work that has influenced many in a "hedge" practice and tradition. For this work, I would posit that the Hedge Druid's Craft stems from a Hedge Witch who has trained in Druid studies, who is free to choose and practice their own tradition and honour the teachings and wisdom gleaned from nature, folklore, history, myth and religion. It is the term "Hedge" that we will investigate more deeply in this work, which may help to further clarify what I mean by the Hedge Druid's Craft. It is about working with boundaries, with a foot in either world, living around the edges and working with liminal times and places. Yes, it is mostly a solitary endeavour, but there is so much more to it.

For all those whose paths meander and often overlap, to those who would not be constrained nor confined by labels, yet who seek some definition, perhaps this work will speak to you. If you are interested in Witchcraft, Wicca or Druidry, I also hope that this book will be of benefit. And to all who walk the wild ways, may we be the awen.

Joanna van der Hoeven
June 2017
www.joannavanderhoeven.com

Introduction from the illustrator

Dear reader, I would like to give you an insight into how I worked on the illustrations in this book. As a Druid I am interested in questing inspiration. I find that the process of co-creating with others is very close to the essence of inspiration or as well call it: Awen. Co-creating takes me into that state where I am listening to someone else, as well as fully being with my own truth. It's like dancing or singing with someone or with a whole group of people.

First of all I read Jo's beautiful words and opened up to the spontaneous flow of feelings, images and associations they invoked in me. I scribbled first sketches on a piece of paper and asked a few questions. That's probably how most artists work, but the next step is a bit more unusual.

Since we are working with the hedge as the main theme of this book, I decided to go out and spend time in the hedge. Using the knowledge I gained through my Druid College apprenticeship I set out on a quest for inspiration. Since I live on a farm I see hedges all the time and I know most of them intimately, as I have repaired the fences along the hedgerows in my work, but this time I decided to meet the boundaries in a different way. I started by going to the oldest oak tree on the farm and sitting under his branches. Becoming still inside I asked the spirits of the place to guide me to a good spot, where I can learn more about the hedge and exchange inspiration. After a few minutes I felt a sense of direction in my body so I started walking, in a timeless state without any fixed destination. To my surprise I discovered areas of the farm that I had never seen before, hidden corners with badger dens, deer tracks and the same vibrant wilderness that I find in the forest. Noticing re-emerging childhood memories and daydreaming about the ancestors, the images and atmospheres started speaking to my soul. I sat down under a hawthorn tree, took out my favourite musical instrument and offered a song to the spirit of the hedge, acknowledging and celebrating its beauty and mystery.

I started sketching whilst sitting in the hedgerow, looking at bramble leaves, nettles and hazel, listening to the little stream and the cars in the background. The first pictures were based on pure observation, but after some time glimpses of the Otherworld pierced through my imagination. A sleepy leaf-and-earth-dragon looked at me from the other side of the stream, ancient stones started humming deep sounding vibrations and friendly birds pointed out certain features of the place that I had not yet noticed. I carried on sketching for most of the day and when I thought I finished my work I closed my eyes and relaxed. Not expecting anything I suddenly felt that someone was sending me a feeling of gratitude. Relaxing deeper, a scene appeared in my mind's eye and I could see a huge white bramble flower held by plant-like hands of a transparent luminous quality. I could feel the sense of delicate care and love that these hands expressed towards the flower. I thought: "Is this a fairy?" then the scene faded away. I have to admit that I don't know the answer to that question and to be honest I don't want to know. In order to enjoy the co-creative process the subjective truth of my experience is enough for me. After offering another song I left the hedge with a bundle of sketches, ready to start working on the final version of the illustrations printed in this book.

What I find so fascinating about the Awen is that it flows so freely from words, to sounds, to images; from humans, to plants, to un-embodied sentient beings and back into words. This sense of an all connecting universal language inspires me to go deeper on my path and give my work as an offering to the Awen.

Yannick Dubois
June 2017
ForestHeart: www.yannickdubois.com

Part One

The Hedge Druid's Craft

Chapter One

Wicca, Witchcraft and Druidry

Witchcraft

Witchcraft is the ability to harness and use the powers of nature and one's own personal energy in order to create a desired effect in the world. It is ancient and found the world over, in various forms under different names and titles. It is often seen as an innate ability, something that one is born with and which may be passed down through generations. We often hear the term "Wise Woman" or "Wise Man" (the "Cunning Folk") to describe a witch practising in her or his community. This would have been someone knowledgeable in herbal healing or midwifery, or speaking with animals, or casting spells and charms or being able to divine the future through weather patterns. In the Middle Ages up until the present moment, Witchcraft was demonised as the Christian faith sought to exude total power and control. However, nature is resilient, and so too were/are Witches. Some of the magic and charms performed have been kept and passed down through folklore and fairy tales. Some lucky families may have kept a tradition alive by passing down wisdom through the bloodline. Though there is no "unbroken lineage" of Witchcraft per se, we can still find fragments and use our instinct and intuition, with the help of guides along the way to enable us to recover and redefine what is often called "The Old Ways". Witchcraft in itself was not known as a religion, but a practice or an art.

Druidry

The Druids of old were tied to the Celtic peoples, and are often equated to the role of priests in the Celtic community. They also held the knowledge and history of their people, genealogy of royal families, poetry, the arts and more. They were often treated as separate and special from the rest of the community, such as being exempt from going to war. Druidry evolved from pre-Celtic religion and spirituality; however, we do not know what that religion or spiritual path was called before the Celts, and so "Druid" is the oldest word which we have to describe a priest of the Celtic tradition that evolved throughout Europe and Britain. The word *Druid* stems from two words, *dru* and *wid*, meaning oak and wisdom respectively. And so, the Druids were seen as those who contained the wisdom of the oak, of nature and the natural world, and who were able to service their communities with their knowledge and their skill. They were an organised elite, as opposed to the village wisewoman/man of Witchcraft. Julius Caesar documents that there were three types of Druids: Bards, Ovates and Druids. Bards held the genealogy, songs and stories of the tribe; Ovates were connected to healing and to seership or divination; and Druids were the teachers, philosophers and those who held the law. Druid schools were in existence up until the seventeenth century. In the nineteenth century interest in the Druids began to re-emerge, in what is often termed "The Celtic Twilight".

Wicca

Wicca and Modern Druidry began in the 1950s. They have their roots and inspiration in the old traditions of Witchcraft and the Druids, yet were formed in order to create branches of a modern Western Paganism that celebrated Nature in all its glory. Two friends, Gerald Gardner and Ross Nichols met around a decade earlier and shared together their mutual interest in magical lore, history and the occult. Gardner published a book called *Witchcraft Today*, and the religion of Wicca was born. Nichols introduced Druidry to the world at large in the mid 1960s, based on the Celtic mythology of Ireland and Britain, history and folklore as well as what he had learned as a member of the Ancient Druid Order. Wicca and Druidry held much in common, as you would imagine, as Gardner and Ross shared so much together in the development of their respective but related paths. Wicca, as the modern formal religion and interpretation of Witchcraft, often contained three degrees, much in the same way that the ancient Druids had the three levels of Bard, Ovate and Druid. Both followed a modern "Wheel of the Year", where ancient festivals and holidays were incorporated into the modern calendar, and rites and rituals created around them to celebrate the seasonal and cyclical nature of the traditions. Wicca and Modern Druidry share much in common, and can be seen as different but related "languages" that express a similar reverence for the cycles of nature, the gods, the ancestors and more. Both have their roots and inspiration in an ancient past, and yet were developed for the modern world to bring back the magic and wonder of nature into everyday life, through rituals and prayer, work and dedication. Wicca is a religion that follows a dual concept of deity, a goddess and god.

Wicca and Witchcraft have often been two terms that were used interchangeably; however, this is now occurring less and less as the traditions seek a distinction between themselves for various reasons. While most Wiccans would say that they are Witches, not all Witches are Wiccans. As stated previously, Witchcraft was not a religion, but a practice. As far as we can tell, there was no dual concept of deity dating back to ancient times. This is a modern interpretation of the forces of nature, which works as a good model for many in the Wiccan tradition. The goddess is all important, and it is her relationship with the god that is the basis for the cyclical and seasonal celebrations. Many Wiccans call this the "Old Religion" stemming from an ancient matriarchal society but this is something of a misnomer. It is largely due to the work of anthropologist Margaret Murray that we have this reasoning which cannot be proven or disproven, hence there is much debate. Murray's work was able to state that Witchcraft was based in a pre-Christian pagan tradition, but to hypothesise further and state that it all derived from a matriarchal Mother Goddess culture is merely just that: a theory. The other modern Wiccan concept of "all the gods are one God, and all the goddesses are one Goddess" is a further theory developed from Murray's work in the late 1970s through the 1990s, mostly promoted by feminist Wiccans such as the brilliant Starhawk. Again, this is not something that has factual basis in an anthropological context, and is hotly contested by many Pagans, whether they are Witches, Wiccans, Druids or from any other tradition. Within Paganism, you will find polytheists (believing in many distinct and separate deities), pantheists (all deities are aspects of a divine force), monotheists (such as the Christian Druids who worship God through nature), or even monists (nature is God). How you choose to incorporate religion, should you wish to in your tradition, is entirely up to you.

And so, Witchcraft is using your wits and intelligence, your own personal power and the powers of nature in order to change the world around you, to affect and effect change. It uses charms and potions, herbal, animal and weather lore, as well as an innate sense of the spirit or energy that dwells in all things. It has an animistic outlook, similar but yet different to Wicca and Druidry.

Wicca focuses on the turning of the Wheel of the Year, often symbolised by the relationship between dual deities, the Goddess and the God. This relationship is reflected in the natural world around us, in the changing of the seasons, in nature and also in human nature. It is a religion as well as a practice.

Druidry focuses more on inspiration, on questing the awen, seeking to find one's place in the human world and the natural world, to live in balance and harmony. It is about becoming a functioning part of an ecosystem, where we understand that all lives are connected; that we are a part of a whole. Some say that Modern Druidry, in relation to Wicca, focuses on the product of the union of the Goddess and God, rather than the relationship between the two.

It is beyond the scope of this work to provide a full and detailed history and all relevant information pertaining to Witchcraft, Wicca and Druidry. To learn more about these traditions, please see the Bibliography and Further Reading at the end of this book, which includes my introduction to Druidry, *The Awen Alone: Walking the Path of the Solitary Druid*.

Re-enchanting our lives is the very reason that Witchcraft, Wicca and Druidry can blend so easily together. Whether you view any of the above as a religion, a philosophy or simply a way of life is irrelevant; what we must acknowledge is that at their core they attempt to honour a pre-Christian tradition, spirituality or practice of Europe and the British Isles. This has been handed down in fragments for us to investigate and reinterpret in order to create beautiful traditions that help us to reweave our connection to the natural world. In today's modern society, we can so often drop the threads of connection, as we live in high-rise apartments, cope with new pressures and stress from a modern society, working eight hours a day while raising our children, and so on. Wicca, Witchcraft and Druidry help us to reconnect to the past while envisioning a future that holds the powers of nature in the highest regard. It is about honouring the cycles of life and death, of transformation and rebirth. It is about re-enchantment, and learning to bring the magic back into our lives. It is about dropping the boundaries between the sacred and the mundane, and truly living magical lives.

Chapter Two

The Hedge – Boundaries and Walking Between the Worlds

The term "hedge" in relation to a spiritual path often simply means that one is not dedicated to any particular path or organisation. However, in an earth-based tradition, the word also takes on a deeper meaning. In a community, there were certain boundaries between the human world and the rest of the natural world. Though we know that we cannot ever be truly separate, still there were and are physical boundaries that we have created over millennia to delineate "our" space from that of others, whether human or non-human. The Hedge Druid's Craft crosses these boundaries and works in both worlds, in all worlds.

Physical Boundaries

Henges and hedges, dill heaps, stone walls and more have marked the edges of a community. In my own little parish, a couple of years ago we re-established "beating the bounds", a tradition of going around and adding soil and sod to the "dill heaps", little mounds of earth that mark the parish boundary. We have two boundaries, one for the lower common and one for the upper common. Looking at old maps, we determined that there were 35 dill heaps for the lower common, and established a day when members of the community could walk the boundaries and search for these little heaps of earth, to reinstate them and to take care of them every two years. It was also the custom to bounce the youngest child on top of each dill heap: why I have no idea! Our vicar blessed the community, the farms and fields, the crops and gardens, the shop and school and then we headed out on a four-mile trek through the landscape. At each dill heap I left an offering of seeds for the local wildlife and the Fair Folk (more about the

Fair Folk later).

To walk a boundary is to find where edges meet. In permaculture, the place where two environments meet, such as forest and field, is where there is the most diversity. Where we find our edges meeting with another, we can gain inspiration, called the *awen* in Druidry. This is what relationship is all about: the give and take, learning and working together, finding out how you fit in your own local patch. The threads of awen shimmer where the edges meet. These are liminal places, where one energy merges with another, such as at the seashore, or on a mountaintop between earth and sky, at the edge of a lake or in a park in the middle of a city.

Hedges are often places that delineate boundaries, and here in Britain there are some hedgerows that are hundreds and hundreds of years old, places of great bio-diversity in an ever-increasing mono-cultured world. Where I live in East Anglia, it is mostly farmland or grazing pasture, and the hedgerows mark the boundaries of the farmer's land. They are also incredible habitats for nature, wonderful "corridors" that allow animals to travel many miles in search of food or places to live. Hedges that link with each other can stretch for miles, and are places where wild birds, mice, snakes, toads, insects of all kinds and more can thrive.

Hedges are also places that can mark the boundary between our garden and the wilderness beyond. I have a hedge all around my back garden, and at the bottom of the garden the hedge marks the spot between me and a small patch of a wild and wooded area that flows along the small valley's depression. Often wild creatures come through holes in the hedge to visit my garden: fallow deer and muntjac deer, badgers, foxes and pheasants. It's also a highway for local cats to pass through into the "wilds" beyond. Yet the hedge is not only a boundary in this very physical sense; it is also a boundary between this world and the Otherworld.

Boundaries Between the Worlds

Physical boundaries such as stone circles or hedges can also delineate a boundary between this world and the Otherworld. In Witchcraft, Wicca and Druidry it is generally acknowledged that there exist beings that are separate from us, yet which also live alongside us in parallel worlds. These beings are often called the Fair Folk, Faeries, the Fey Folk, The Good Folk, the Tuatha de Danaan, The Little People, The Gentry and more. These are creatures often connected to a place, or sometimes seen as nature spirits. They are even more vast and diverse than the human race. They live in a world that straddles ours, and here in Britain there are certain times of the year when it is said that the veil between the worlds is thin. These are times when we can easily cross over into the Otherworld, and they can come in to ours. The tides of Beltane and Samhain, (May Day and Hallowe'en) are when the boundaries are at their most "open". Other times of the year, such as the solstices, have folklore and legends too regarding portals between this realm and the realms of Faerie.

One Beltane a being of the Fair Folk came through the hole in the hedge at the bottom of my garden. The energy of our Beltane ritual still hung in the air, shimmering in the light of the full moon. I was now alone in the garden, tidying up the lanterns and getting ready to put the fire to bed. As I walked down the garden steps, my offering of milk and honey in my hands, I made my way across the lawn to where the altar and offering place lay beneath the canopy of an old beech, its leaves just beginning to bud. I said a quick prayer as I entered that sacred space, with nine small stones delineating the boundary of this "faerie circle", a "minilithic" stone circle I had built for meditation and ritual purposes.

As I walked into the circle, I felt the air thick with the magic of the evening. I knew something was about to happen. I laid the food and drink upon the altar, and gave my thanks to the spirits of place, and to the Fair Folk. No sooner had the words left my mouth than a rustling in the hedge all around me began. It was as if some strange wind was shaking just the coniferous boundary of my garden, or a small army of badgers were all coming through the little holes in the hedge at the same time. My heart pounded in my chest as the moon shone through the branches of the beech above me. Frozen in place, both excited and frightened to see what happened next, I tried to see into the darkness of the hedge, shadowed from the moon's light, but I could perceive nothing but the inky blackness.

The rustling all around me stopped, and I found I was able to move. I knew that something had come through the hole in the hedge, but I could not see it. Slowly I walked towards the firepit, hoping to see what had come through by the light of the fire. I cautiously approached the dying flames, and peered into the shadows about ten feet away. I could see very little, but I felt a presence, someone – male – standing by the birdfeeder and the hole in the hedge, shoulder-height to me, dressed in shades of brown. Suddenly, even as I looked and felt his presence, he moved without a sound like a dark shadow in the blink of an eye back into the hedge, and there from the depths of the green and black two eyes shone a whitish/green, reflecting the light of the fire. Whatever that being was, he had changed into the form of a badger in the blink of an eye, to watch me from the depths of the back hedgerow.

"Beltane blessings," I murmured. Unsure of what to do next and still very much afraid and alone, I curtseyed and then covered the firepit with its iron mesh guard, walking back slowly towards the house. I had wanted to ask for his friendship, and for that of all the Fair Folk, but my courage failed me on that night of the full moon, as the powers of Beltane and the Otherworld flowed through the land.

Hedge Riding

Hedges have long been used by Witches in the community, who were often termed "Hedge Riders". They were those who worked between the boundaries of the everyday and those of the wilderness; the wild spirits that dwelt therein. It is about finding the balance between our modern civilized world and that of the natural world. This too is often the inspiration for many in Druidry and Wicca. The German word "hagazissa" means "hedge sitter", who was a person who could go between the worlds, travel beyond the human settlement and the places of the wild spirits and the Otherworld, bringing back information, healing and more to the community. They were able to "ride" that delineating line between the human world and the Otherworld. The Saxon term is "haegtessa" and both words are where we get our word "hag" from, now often relating to a witch of a certain age.

Hedge Riding can be done to connect with the spirit of nature, or to travel across different realms. In this work, I present the Otherworld using a Celtic motif of the World Tree, which will be discussed later. This is the tree that we will "ride" up and down, to connect to the Otherworld, its guides and its mysteries.

The journey of personal transformation is never an easy one. Living a life dedicated to earth-based spirituality, to working in the Hedge Druid's Craft, often alone and without support other than your wits and the wisdom your guides can provide, is a challenging one in today's modern times. We can often feel so distanced from everyone around us. I get those moments, when I'm in my village shop, or walking down a street and think, "*I'm so different from everyone else. There are so few people out there in this world that think and care about the things I do.*" It can seem a lonely and distancing way of being, I'll tell you. But then I take a deep breath, perhaps say a quick prayer to my goddess, remember my encounters with the Fair Folk and feel the strength of my ancestors at my back. And I know that the work that I do has meaning, that I have given my life meaning. Remember, the meaning of life is to give your life meaning. And if you honour the gods, the ancestors, the spirits of place, the earth and the universe itself, and you truly *do* the work, then your life has a deeper meaning than most can ever achieve. (Not that this is a competition, mind you.)

Chapter Three

The World of the Hedge Druid

The World of the Hedge Druid's Craft

The world of the Hedge Druid's Craft is one where we take inspiration from nature, and allow traditional folk customs, history and mythology to blend with the powers of nature so that we can better work in harmony. As we walk between the worlds, we open ourselves up to the wisdom of plants, animals and the forces of weather around us that influence us each and every day. We can use and harness this wisdom to help our own lives, the lives of those in our community, and the world at large. When we open ourselves to the realms of plants, animals and weather, we broaden our horizons, literally and figuratively. We work on both sides of the hedge, the civilized and the wild, and also within the hedge, the liminal place, in our work.

The Hedge Druid's Craft is found in liminal places. This is a place that is "in between" places: the place where the hedge meets the field, the high tide line on the seashore, a clearing in a forest. You can also work at a liminal time: dusk or dawn, in the twilight hours where it is not quite day, nor night, or when the tide is turning from low to high and vice versa. What matters most is that you are working from the edge, seeking to connect to that which is Other.

The Hedge Druid's Craft is also that which seeks out the lore of the surrounding countryside. That means researching local folklore, as well as walking the land as much as you can, getting to know the land and allowing the land to know you. It is researching old magical traditions, potions, charms and spells and uses them as inspiration for your own work. For example, here in Suffolk, in the UK, where I live there are ancient Celtic sites that I visit to do my work, using the energy and assistance of the ancestors. There are the remains of an ancient oak woodland nearby, which is a truly magical realm in and of itself. There are ancient green roads that countless feet have walked, and ley lines that begin in Cornwall and pass through this land to come and flow into the North Sea. There are tales of Suffolk witches, moats that hold power, and ghostly goings on that give us a clue as to past traditions, lifestyle and country temperament that can inspire the Hedge Druid's Craft today. There are also local traditions, such as the Horseman's Society which flourished in East Anglia, and which also has links to the endangered Suffolk Punch breed of horses. The Horseman's Society's ways are reputed to hold the magic of witches and retained relics of the area's pagan past, enabling one to communicate and charm an animal without resorting to force. There are enormous black dogs that roam the heathland, and mystery houses that appear and disappear, such as the mansion near Little Welnetham by the church of Bradfield St George. There are also tales of encounters with the Otherworld and the Fair Folk, such as the popular folk tale of the Green Children of Woolpit, who were found wandering the countryside, their skin as green as the leaves on the trees, and who slowly changed to a normal human colour after being adopted and raised by locals. And we cannot forget the historical record of one of the nastiest men in English history, Matthew Hopkins, Witchfinder General and the atrocities that he committed throughout the countryside.

Knowing your local area, its history and its tales, helps with the Hedge Druid's Craft to develop a real sense of place, and inspires one to continue an ancient tradition in up to date ways for a modern world. Inspired by the past, we can work towards creating balance between the worlds, in our local patch, and in our soul.

The Seasonal Festivals

The Hedge Druid's Craft honours the seasonal festivals, and can work with the four quarter/agricultural festivals of Imbolc, Beltane, Lughnasadh and Samhain. She can also work with the four cross-quarter days: the spring and autumn equinox, and the winter and summer solstice. The modern Pagan Wheel of the Year was designed to incorporate all eight festivals, so that something was celebrated roughly every six to eight weeks. This keeps us modern folk attuned to what is happening in the natural world around us, both in the wilds and in the farmers' fields, in the lanes and in the hedgerows.

The eight festivals and their corresponding times are:

- Samhain – sunset of 31st October to sunset 1st November. If working by the moon, it is the first full moon when the sun is in Scorpio. If working by the natural landscape, it is when the first frosts bite. Samhain was termed the Celtic New Year, as it marked the ending of one cycle and the beginning of another. The Celts reckoned their days from sunset to sunset, and so the start of the year would begin in the dark time at the beginning of winter. Samhain marked the first day of winter.

- Winter Solstice – falling sometime between 20th to 22nd December, can change year upon year. Marks the mid-way point of Celtic winter, hence often called Mid-Winter Solstice. It is the time of the longest night and shortest day. Three days after this solstice, the sun begins to rise and set further north on the horizon. It was a time of celebration at the returning of the light, and the lengthening days.

- Imbolc – sunset of 31st January to sunset 1st February. If working by the moon, it is the first full moon when the sun is in Aquarius. If working by the natural landscape, it is when the ewes begin to lactate as the lambing season begins, or when the first snowdrops appear. Imbolc was an important time, for it heralded the first signs of the end of winter. Fresh milk was now available to supplant the meagre and dwindling winter stores, so fresh butter and cheeses could keep the community going until other food became available.

- Spring Equinox – falling sometime between 20th to 22nd March, can change year upon year. Marks the time when the days become longer than the nights. It is a time when nature starts to show her bounty, as daffodils bloom, nettles become proficient once again, and wild food begins to appear once more in the hedgerows. Fields were sown around this time.

- Beltane – sunset of 30th April to sunset 1st May. If working by the moon, it is the first full moon when the sun is in Taurus. If working by the natural landscape, it is when the hawthorn tree comes into bloom. This marked the beginning of summer for the Celts, when cattle were taken from their winter lodging and into their summer pastures, often cited as being driven between two bonfires for purification (and to get rid of fleas, ticks and other nasties). It was a time of fertility, when the fields began to show their bounty, and gatherings and festivals were held in honour of many courtships.

- Summer Solstice – 20th to 22nd of June can change year upon year. Marks the mid-point of summer in the Celtic calendar, hence often called Mid-Summer. It is the time of the longest day and the shortest night. Three days after this solstice, the sun begins to rise and set further south on the horizon. It was a celebration of the greatest light, and a reflection on the coming autumn and winter.

- Lughnasadh – sunset of 31st July to 1st August. If working by the moon, it is the first full moon when the sun is in Leo. If working by the natural landscape, it is when the first crop of wheat is harvested. This often marked the beginning of the harvest season, and can be viewed as the beginning of autumn. Many myths and folklore surround the harvesting of the first crop, such as keeping the last sheaf and making a corn dolly to ensure the blessing of fertility for a good crop in the following year.

- Autumn Equinox – falling sometime between 20th and 22nd September, can change year upon year. Marks the time when the nights become longer than the days, and we shift into the winding down of the year. Often called Harvest Home in the UK, many local parishes still celebrate this with community gatherings. More crops are being taken in, and the sounds of the combine harvester can be heard long into the night.

This is a brief overview of the eight festivals. The Hedge Druid's Craft is mainly based on locality, and so to see the changing of the seasons in relation to the eight festivals is a great way to keep in tune with nature and her wonder. For those who don't live in the countryside, having these times marked can remind us of what our ancestors celebrated, and what is happening beyond the confines of human urbanisation.

Rite to Enter the World of the Hedge Druid's Craft

This rite can be used to dedicate yourself to The Hedge Druid's Craft, to walking between the worlds. If you can, begin your work by standing in or near a hedgerow itself, looking away from civilisation. If this is not possible, you can create a hedgerow by standing between two plants. Many potted trees will do well indoors, so you can research their properties and see what kind would be suited to your work. Stand on your dominant leg, raising your non-dominant foot off the ground (if you are right-handed, then your dominant side is your right side, for example). Close your non-dominant eye, perhaps by placing your non-dominant had over that eye. This is a very tricky pose to hold for long, and if you are in a public place, can look rather odd. It is, however, an ancient Druid pose used to travel between the worlds, as one half of you is solid and grounded, while the other half is being suspended. If this is too difficult a pose to maintain for any period of time, you can just put your non-dominant foot forward, to symbolise "walking

between the worlds". Or you can hold the more difficult pose for a few seconds, before moving to the easier pose.

Whatever pose you choose to use, hold it for a few moments until you feel a shift in consciousness, then say these or similar words:

I walk between the worlds, by the blessings of nature:
By the blessing of the green and growing things
By the blessing of the wild creatures
By the blessing of the Fair Folk.
I walk the path of the Hedge Druid's Craft;
May the wisdom of the Otherworld be open to me;
May I take my guidance from all the realms around me
In safety and surety I travel between the worlds
To speak in the language of bird and beast
Of plant and rock
Of the sun and moon and stars.

Turn anti-clockwise three times, and state:

By the power of three times three
This is my will, so may it be.

Take a moment to adjust, and know that wherever you go, whether you choose to move from this space or not, you are now also in the Otherworld. Here, you can receive guidance from plants and animals, from nature spirits and the Fair Folk, from gods and goddesses of the wild wood and more.

Journey where you wish to go. This can be done either in the physical realm, actually walking across heathland or meadow, or through a forest, or down the beach. Know that you are straddling the worlds as you walk, and that what you see and come across may have a very different meaning than in ordinary reality. Or you can simply sit where you have begun the rite, and journey in your mind to a place where you wish to travel, to gain wisdom from the plants and animals, the ancestors and other guides you may meet. Start slowly and gently, becoming used to being between the worlds. It is not something to be rushed, but to be savoured.

When you have finished, return back to the place where you began, and assume the original posture once again, this time facing towards civilisation. Say these or similar words:

I return from walking between the worlds;
In harmony and in peace I return.
May my powers be strengthened,
May I receive protection in all my endeavours
As I work towards balance and harmony with the whole.
May I be the awen (inspiration).

Turn clockwise three times, and state:

By the power of three times three
This is my will, so may it be.

Take a moment to settle back into this world. If you can, eat and drink something to ground you in the present moment. You might clap your hands three times, or pat the earth three times to signal your full return. You can also say your name aloud three times. Journal your experience as soon as you are able.

This beginning rite can be performed each time you begin your work in walking between the worlds, in hedge riding. You might do this before you go out to collect plants for your work, or to search for guidance from animal companions, or to use the weather to predict future events. It helps you to bring magic back into your life, to re-enchant the soul. When simple actions are performed when one is between the worlds, the power is increased and the work which we do sings out in a chorus of harmony across the web of all existence.

Chapter Four

The Ancestors

The ancestors are a very important part of the Druid tradition. They have a lot to do with our moral and ethical framework. As we realise the interconnectedness of all things, we come to the point where we know that we are all related. We all came from the single-celled life forms that emerged from the oceans all those years ago. We have a shared ancestry. We also know that the world of the living is built upon the world of the dead. We cannot have life without death. The soil that we grow our food on is made of decomposed plant and animal matter, and so we honour the ancestors each and every day simply for the earth that we walk on, the food that we eat. We know that without the ancestors, without those who have gone before, we simply would not be.

However, most often when we are working with the ancestors, we think of our human ancestors. This might be because we can relate to our human ancestors perhaps more easily than we can to those single-celled organisms. We still honour the fact that we would not exist were it not for all our ancestors, but for many the focus lies on human ancestry, and that is perfectly fine, as long as we remember our shared ancestry with all life forms.

In Druidry, with our human ancestors there are three different strands. We have ancestors of blood: those human ancestors with whom we are directly related. Yes, we are all related to each other if you go back far enough, but our blood ancestors help to narrow down the group a little bit in order to find a number that we can actually function with on a more intimate level. So do we honour our parents and grandparents, our great grandparents and so on, as far back as we can remember their names and their history. For their stories are also our stories, and their stories flow through our veins. If you are adopted, then you have two bloodlines from which you can work. You can honour your blood relatives, if you choose to discover who they are. You can also honour the bloodline of your adoptive parents. You may want to work with both at the same time.

The second set of ancestors which we work with is the ancestors of place. These are the ancestors of our locality. Working in the Hedge Druid's Craft, we need to learn the local history and geography of the place we call home. In doing so, we come to a deeper understanding of the place, and of our place within that place, if you see what I mean. The ancestors of place are those who have gone before and who have lived upon this land.

The third set of ancestors honoured in the Druid tradition are the ancestors of tradition, those spiritual ancestors whose faith, belief, work or person has inspired others on their journey. These could be modern-day Druids, Wiccans or Pagans who do great work in the community, or a teacher that we remember fondly who inspired us in our school years. It could be a religious figure, such as Gandhi or Mother Teresa, or from any other tradition, such as the Buddha. It could be an artist who inspires us, or a poet, scientist or musician.

If we look at the bigger picture, we can also bring a fourth strand of ancestors to the mix. These are the ancestors of the future, those who will carry on after we have passed away. These might be blood relatives, or they might not be. These are simply those who will inherit the world that we give them. When we consider our ancestors of the future, as well as being guided by ancestors of blood, place and tradition, then our Craft is deeply rooted in time, in place, and in a deep sense of wakefulness.

To connect with your blood ancestors, you can do the following exercise as a meditation.

Close your eyes, and focus on your breath.

Choose a bloodline to follow, whether from your mother's or father's side. Choose a single parent, and envision them standing behind you. You can feel their presence behind you, and a line that links your heart to theirs. As you breathe, you breathe together, that line also linking your breath. Breathe with each other for a moment.

Now, see your parent's parents, standing behind your parent, with a connecting thread to your parent from their hearts, which then connects to you through your parent. Breathe with them, all three generations breathing together.

Now envision your grandparents' parents, and their parents, back throughout the mists of time. Even if you don't know their faces, feel their presence behind you, stretching back and connecting to each other, breathing together through that single thread from your heart.

Now, turn to face your ancestors, acknowledging them, breathing with them.

Spend a moment just breathing with your ancestors, and then listen to the message that your ancestors have to tell you.

Now turn away, but still feel all your ancestors behind you, breathing with you. Know that they are a part of you, and will always be a part of you.

And slowly, with each inhale, allow your ancestors to fade from your view, but not from your consciousness; generation by generation, until you stand alone once more. Though they are gone from your vision, they still live on in your heart, and in your breath.

Focus on your own breath once more, and slowly begin to be aware of the sounds around you. Wiggle your fingers and toes, and when you are ready, open your eyes.

Chapter Five

The Gods

In Druidry and in Wicca, the gods are a part of nature, as are we, flowing through time and space. That quality, that energy that we term as deity is within everything. As it is within everything, nothing is better than anything else. There is an inherent animism within Druidry, insomuch as we know that one thing is not better than another, that everything has its own inherent value. It is something that we work with every day, coming up against our own notions of value, where we place the boundaries of our knowledge and experience upon the world. When we have lost sight of the sacred, we look to other distractions in order to stave off the fear and longing of self-imposed separation.

The gods are energy; the gods are immanent. They take on whatever form they wish, or whatever form we feel we are best able to communicate with and establish a relationship in order to learn and understand. The gods may hold more power in certain regards than we do; for example, as a thunderstorm raging across the landscape may hold terrible power, causing floods and damage to many homes, both human and other than human. But we also have that power within ourselves, the tides that flood through us, our capacity for creation and destruction. We simply act upon those tides to create *harmony* within our ecosystem as much as we can, for that is the purpose of the Hedge Druid's Craft. The earth knows what She is doing, and so storms and earthquakes happen. The earth, as all beings are, is constantly seeking homeostasis, the balance point. We can see the destruction of the storm, but we can also see the need for that storm to have happened, the part that we played in causing it, such as through global warming and climate change. Though the gods may appear terrible and mighty, they are not *better* than us, just different.

Equally, the world over has deities of love and compassion, of empathy and peace. These deities are not better than us, but serve as an example of how we too can work with their energy in order to create a harmonious union with everything around us. Just as we don't hold a person or a celebrity higher than ourselves simply because they exist, neither do we do so for any deity. We are simply working with them, using the notion of co-operation and co-existence in order to live our lives in service to our Craft.

I think it's important that we learn how to be in the world without losing our power, our autonomy. All too readily we are willing to give authority and power over to a teacher, a celebrity, a god, and in doing so we are doing a disservice to ourselves. It's fine to respect people for what they say and more importantly for what they do, but we must also learn to stand on our own two feet and be the light that we want to see in the world. I've done it several times in the past, giving up my power to a teacher, a boss, a partner, whatever. Often when we meet people we admire, we lose ourselves: we forget our own inherent self-worth. Just because someone has something to say, perhaps even something important, doesn't make them better than you. Just because someone knows more things than you do, doesn't make them better than you. We all know different things. Just because someone has had life experience, doesn't make them better than you. A child is just as important as an octogenarian. Don't give up your power to anyone. Admire them, sure, respect them, but do not place them on any sort of pedestal. The gods included.

But what makes a god, a god? How can we differentiate between something that is, say, the sidhe or fairy, or a spirit of place, from a god?

We humans are always so keen to label things, to put them in boxes, but really we need to do this to an extent in order to grasp some concepts that at first may seem far too large to handle. If we look at the spirits of place, this is the energy of a location. It is also viewed as the energy of the land, the sea or the sky. For me, it's all about locality. I honour the spirits of place where I live: the beech tree in the backyard, the blackbirds and the pheasants, the deer that come through the hole in the hedge at the bottom of the garden. Everything that is in my locality can be considered a spirit of place. There is often a fine distinction between a god and the spirit of place, and that line can move about from entity to entity. My teacher once said that divinity or deity is a force of nature that has the power to kill. Therefore, a river, a storm, a flood, the sun, the process of birthing and dying: these are all gods. They are all a part of nature. There are also gods of human nature as well: gods of lust and rage, love and ecstasy. For me, I feel this definition is still too limited; I feel that deity is something which operates on a much grander scale, whether or not it has the capacity to kill us. So, I honour the spirits of place where I live, but the over-arching energy that holds it all together, say, the heathland in its entirety as delineated by natural boundaries, is to me a god. The forest that lies to the north of the heathland is, to me, a god. It would be difficult for the heath or forest to kill me; I might get bitten by an adder if I am not careful walking about in the sunshine, but the adder is simply a part of that greater energy, and not the energy itself. Perhaps we can even see human beings as being a part of the greater energy of a god, or God if you want to use a capital "G". My teacher later described god as nature, and that, I think, hits closer to the mark for me. It is more the path of the mystic, to be sure, but it still encompasses the feeling that God or the gods are something other than ourselves, bigger than ourselves, but still comprised of ourselves.

Ascribing gender to a god is yet another way for the human mind to grasp such a large concept as a god or a goddess, and is all part of helping us to relate that power, to that energy. Maybe one day we will lose the idea of gender altogether, in society and in relation to the gods. It's a personal thing. In my work, some gods of the gods I work with have no gender, such as the god of the heathland. I'm not sure if the forest has a gender. But my lady

Brighid I see as female.

It might be concerned with having ancestral gods, as well as finding out the gods of your own locality. With ancestral, named gods, we are using all the past associations that have come with them through the mists of time. We are also perhaps giving them new associations. Brighid, for me, can also be seen as the goddess of technology, the spark of electricity. Because she has been seen as a woman for thousands of years, I find that I can reach back through my own human heritage to know her as such, as my ancestors did thousands of years ago. But really, when it all comes down to it, she is simply energy. Much as we are.

Everything that exists and has ever existed is simply energy given form. Some we see, some we can't. We know the power and energy that the wind has, but we cannot see it; we can only see its effects on the environment. When it comes to beings such as humans, or other animals, we know that we are comprised of countless atoms bouncing off each other, moving and creating energy, that spirals upwards in layers of energy bound to a manifest form. The table in front of me is energy given form. Though I can't see that energy, what gives the table its solidity is the fact that atoms moving around are sustaining the manifest form that I know as "wood". We also know that energy moves *through* things as well, through "solid" things. There are atoms that can move through this table, through walls, through the human body. Physics is a wonderful way to realise the true interconnectedness of all life.

So, for me, the gods are a collection of energy that is larger than the spirits of place, yet made up of the spirits of place. It is a powerful energy that we can connect to. If we look at it from a monist perspective, nature is god and god is nature. That simplifies things to an extent, but may make it harder to relate to as it operates on such a grand scale. That is why we have polytheists, those who work with many separate gods in Druidry and in Wicca, as well as monists. There are also atheist druids, those who see Druidry as a philosophy rather than a religion. Wicca is a religion that has a goddess and a god as its core tenet, though they may not be named specifically. Some Witches don't work with deity at all.

In order to delve deeply into that energy, I search for the gods to work with, to inspire me. I need that connection in my life. For others, they don't. To each their own.

Ancestral gods are gods from a people or a tribe that have moved from one place to another. Indeed, many of the Celtic gods can be seen as ancestral gods. Take Brighid, for example. She was known to many people all across Britain and Ireland, and also across Europe. She may well have been a deity with Indo European roots, migrating with the Celts when they travelled across Europe to these isles, and even beyond to America. In some parts of Europe she was known as Brig or Brigu, in France she was known as Brigitae or Brigantia. She was also known as Brigantia to the northern Brigantes tribe in England, who took their name after her. In Scotland, she is known as Brighde, Brigh, Bridean and Bridi. In Wales, she is known as Ffraid, Bregit, Braint and by many other names. In Ireland, she is known as Brighid, Brigit, Brigid or Saint Brigid. She has even travelled to America to mingle with the Voudon religion, where she is known as Madame Brigitte or Maman Brigitte. She has an energy, a quality, that seems to travel with her that correlates to the places where her people settled. A deity of fire and water, of healing, of poetry and smithcraft, she can find a place amongst many localities. Ancestral deities are found the world over.

Later in this book we will enter into a rite to meet with the gods and gain inspiration for our highest potential on our spiritual path.

Chapter Six

The Fair Folk (Sidhe)

The people of the mounds, those who live in the hollow hills, are held within the earth's deep embrace. These are often known as the Fair Folk, Faerie or the Sidhe: the inhabitants of the realms of Faerie. We can travel to their world through special entrances at special times of the year, some more easily than others. The veils are said to be particularly thin at the festivals of Samhain and Beltane. We can use the axis mundi, the World Tree, to move between the worlds, and we will do so later in this book.

We're often taught from childhood in today's society that the faerie folk are in our imagination only. But as we walk further down the Druid path, we realise that there is more than what we can perceive with our dulled physical senses. Hopefully, we will have opened up our awareness in seeking a path of the Hedge Druid's Craft, and come to an understanding that there is more than what conventional society tells us exists. We may even begin to believe in faeries.

Perhaps even the word "belief" is not quite accurate in this context. We begin to know, rather than believe. We have enchanted our world by opening our perception to it. Enchantment – *en chantement* – is French for "to sing into". We begin to hear other songs, songs other than our own. We sing our own song back, and find where we are in the great song. There, we find no need for belief.

Most Druid traditions will work with aspects of Faery, as do many Wiccan traditions. Coming as it does from a Celtic tradition, these fair folk feature prominently in the myths and stories of the Celtic people. The Celtic term "Sidhe" literally translates as "The People from the Hollow Hills". Dr. James Maertens in the *8th Mount Haemus Lecture, Entering Faerie – Elves, Ancestors &*

Imagination states:

> It is evident that some people possess "the Sight" either temporarily or without being particularly aware of it, as encounters with these "invisible" persons or creatures are relatively rare. Thus two characteristics of the denizens of Faerie are (1) that they can appear and disappear in a way that is uncanny to human senses, and (2) their contacts with mortal humans are rare enough to make good stories around the fire.
>
> We have stories from ancestors old and new and from our contemporaries, who have given us accounts of their communication and sightings of the Hidden People. In addition to older legends and romances, scholars have written down many oral accounts over the past two hundred years. Some of these are given as first-person accounts, some second-hand, and some as literary accounts that take the form of mythic or legendary narratives, or as fantasy literature. It is important to note that I do not consider any of these categories to be more true than others. One does not have to label one story true and another false, even if they contradict each other in many points. Nor do I privilege first-hand oral tales over literary creations. They are all stories created through the human imagination and only the authors of those stories can tell to what extent they believe themselves to have been inspired by communication with the denizens of Faerie. I suspect that many who write literary tales of the Otherworlds are in fact inspired by true visions of those worlds, whether they know it or not. The process of Imbas or inspiration is mysterious.

Making the pilgrimage to a physical area is an act of dedication in and of itself. When I began my relationship with the Fair Folk or the Sidhe, I often travelled to a special place of power near me that is an ancient Celtic tumuli. It's a five- to six-mile round trip for me either by foot or on bicycle to this ancient site. But I made it fairly regularly, for I wished to establish a relationship with the place and its inhabitants.

Once there, I would calm and attune myself to the place, listening to the birds, the sheep on the heath below, the wind through the trees. There are several old oaks and sweet chestnut trees that grow on and around the tumuli. I would sit beneath their branches and settle, and then reach deep into the ground with my mind, sometimes envisioning myself as a tree, sending my taproot deep into the earth and bringing up the nourishment to fill my soul. With eyes closed, I then would call to the Sidhe in my mind, asking for them to make themselves known to me, so that I may feel their presence. They often responded, most of the time, though not always.

I would feel their presence around me. Still sitting with eyes closed, I would feel them standing around me, their tall, ethereal, shining forms looking down on me as I sat cross-legged on the earth. They sometimes talked to me, they sometimes simply talked to each other about me, but I could feel their presence. When I opened my eyes, they were still there, but even more ethereal; I could barely see them. So, with eyes closed I would focus more intently upon them, as I sat upon the earth, next to or on the tumuli on the hill.

They are often curious, and usually helpful. Sometimes they are cryptic, sometimes straightforward. But they are always there, a part of time and space. I travel to meet them physically and mentally, and through their entrance to the Lowerworld I see them, meet with them, letting them experience me even as I experience them.

I can take my experiences at the tumuli back home with me as well. In ritual, I can drum and journey within my mind back to that physical location, whereupon I can have a similar experience. If I have a question that needs answering, I can seek it there. Likewise, I can seek information or a different perception. But whether I travel in person to this spot, or in my mind, the Fair Folk are always there. We must, in the Hedge Druid's Craft, make the journey for ourselves, if we can, both in our minds and in the world. Only then will we truly learn integration of the seen and unseen, the experience transforming our knowledge into wisdom. Find a place that you can visit where you feel the call of the Fair Folk to be the strongest. There will be power spots around you, at liminal places where the practice of the Hedge Druid's Craft feels most comfortable. Seek these out, come to know them and let them come to know you. Later in this book is a rite that can be used to meet with the Fair Folk, to befriend them and allow them to guide you in your Craft.

Part Two

The World Tree

The Three Worlds and the World Tree

In the Hedge Druid's Craft, we work with the concept of the World Tree, which is divided into three realms: the Lowerworld, Middleworld and Upperworld. As we like to use the hedge motif, when we are "hedge riding" we are riding along the axis of the World Tree, travelling between the worlds.

As Druids, who seek the wisdom of the oak, using a tree motif can be wholly appropriate to the path. According to ancient sources, the Druids celebrated in groves (sacred nemetons), and trees were very important to their religious and spiritual tradition. Some Druids use this tree motif in connection with the worlds, others see them as circles or spheres within spheres, interconnecting. These three worlds are sometimes referred to as Annwn (or Ceugant as Iolo Morgannwg named it), Abred and Gwynfed.

Accessing the three worlds through the centre, the axis mundi, (the *Bile* in Irish) is the trunk of the Middleworld that connects all three and is how we are able to move between the worlds. We will look at introductory rites and rituals that allow us to travel up and down the tree, to ride the hedge and to travel between the worlds later in the section.

Chapter Seven

The Lowerworld (Annwn)

Annwn translates as "in-world" or "the very deep place". The translation of "Ceugant" most roughly approximates "infinity", or finding or returning to some sort of "source" or "god". It is found at the base of the World Tree, deep within its roots. It's a place of mystery, of power, memory and grounding. In the Hedge Druid's Craft, if we look to the wisdom of the oak, we know that the roots of an oak tree extend as far beneath the ground as branches overhead, with the trunk as the middle ground between the two, connecting and supporting them. This knowledge can be applied to the three worlds of the Lower, Middle and Upper, positing that each world is as important as the other, and that what is hidden only reflects what is apparent.

The Underworld holds the memories of our ancestors, of generations upon generations of beings that have made up the soil that carries life to us today. It is a place of quiet mystery and deep power. It is also the domain of spiritual beasts, and of a stag headed god who guards the Well of Segais. It is not a place of fear or condemnation, but rather a place where transformation and knowledge work hand in hand to allow things to come out into the light.

Annwn held the cauldron of transformation, which was warmed by the breath of nine maidens. It is often equated with the feminine, however, the Dagda, that wonderfully lusty and great god, had a cauldron of his own, from which one could come back to life. His cauldron was called Undry, or the Cauldron of Plenty. Deep in the Underworld, within Annwn we can rest, contact the ancestors, and find transformation through the slow process of warming our own cauldron of potential. It is where the physical is broken down, much like vegetable matter is broken down into compost, to become something that can nourish and sustain us.

The Underworld or Annwn is also often equated to the lands of the Sidhe. The term *sidhe* can be a difficult one, as it can mean so many things, from a faerie or fey type being, to an ancestor. In the Welsh/British tradition, the Sidhe lived in hollow hills, and so by travelling into the hills and going deep into the land, we find Otherworlds of great magic. Not always a place of darkness, when we travel to these places we might find worlds that mirror our own, bright as day or dark as midnight. Often they are described as neither day nor night, as having no sunrise and no sunset. Time does not move the same there as it does in the Middleworld, the world where we spend most of our time. We can journey to the Underworld by travelling down into the roots of the World Tree.

Connecting to the Lowerworld

The Lowerworld is often associated with the Sidhe, the Fair Folk, the faerie folk. Travelling by means of the World tree, we can work with the Fair Folk as well as the ancestors in the Lowerworld. The ability to be open, to open our perception, is key to travelling between the worlds. We also have some ritual tools to hand, such as the staff or wand (which symbolises the World Tree), herbs, charms, potions and more which can help us on our journey (for more on ritual tools, please read my introductory book *The Crane Bag: A Druid's Guide to Ritual Tools and Practices*). Each person's journey will be different, each person's encounter with Faerie unique. We will each perceive these beings in a different way, as we ourselves are perceived as different from each other. The one constant that remains is that these beings exist the world over, throughout cultures and religions all across our planet. There is a shamanistic thread that binds humanity together, which is not primitive, not simple or reductionist, but simply unifying in its weave. As Corby Ingold writes in the essay "Shamanism in the Celtic World" (OBOD website):

The final problem remaining to us is identifying the Celtic

shaman. We have no word from ancient Celtic tradition that is exactly cognate with the word "shaman", though there are plenty of terms for religious and magical practitioners of various types. Some scholars have suggested the Old Irish word fili, meaning a kind of poet/seer, as the likely term for a shaman in ancient Irish society. Opinions on this are, however, far from unanimous. Without knowing what an ancient Celtic shaman might have been called within whichever of the Celtic societies he existed in, and precisely how his role as a shaman was defined within those societies, it is very difficult to say with any certainty that there were Celtic shamans.

We can say with some certainty, however, that shamanic elements are to be found within Celtic tradition from ancient to modern times, and back up our assertion with prominent examples such as those given here. For the modern spiritual seeker or shamanic practitioner seeking a connection with Celtic roots, there is a wealth of rich material to explore in several languages, existing in books both ancient and modern. There is, in addition, research to be done among living Celtic peoples and lands. And ultimately, there is the Land herself upon which our Celtic ancestors lived, and upon which their descendants yet live today. If we empty ourselves, and go to Her, and seek in the silence to hear Her voice, she will speak to us as she spoke to those ancient and far flung wanderers.

In the Hedge Druid's Craft, we can seek relationship with the Fair Folk, the Faeries, the Sidhe, deep within the Hollow Hills. We can seek them out, using our wit and intelligence, our skills and knowledge, if we dare. We can connect to the Lowerworld through their means, through their places of power, through the gateways that we begin to perceive, both seen and unseen. We can, through the aid of allies such as the ancestors, and other spirit guides establish a deeper connection to the sidhe, and enter into a relationship with the Lowerworld that enriches our lives and enchants our souls.

Find a tree near you that you can visit regularly. Spend some time with your tree, which you will be using to help you journey to the Lowerworld. Befriend the tree. Research all that you can, enlighten yourself as to its ways. You will only learn by doing the work.

To enter the Lowerworld and connect with an ancestral or Faerie guide, you can use a rite such as the one that follows, which ideally should be performed out of doors, but if that is impossible, can be done indoors as instructed previously using indoor potted trees as your liminal place, taking the place of an outdoor hedge.

Go to your special, liminal place, whether that be a hedge, the seashore, the forest edge, a mountaintop or a park in a city, or to a tree with whom you have a special relationship. Assume the Druidic pose, the one-legged "within this world and the other" posture described previously, or simply place your non-dominant foot forward. Notice how this posture makes you feel, and stay with it for as long as you wish, to allow your consciousness to move from the world of the civilized to the world of nature. When you are ready, say the following or similar words:

I walk between the worlds with the World Tree as my guide;
May my roots reach deep,
May my core be strong and centred, and
May my inspiration reach towards the skies.
I now venture into the Lowerworld
To understand my deepest shadow,
To seek the roots of any difficulty,
And to find my spirit guide as Ancestor or Fair Folk.
In the realms below I search out my inner truth
To bring it back into the Middleworld.
May I be aided in this endeavour
By those who are attuned with my intention.

Turn around counter-clockwise three times, and say:

By the power of three times three,
This is my will, so may it be.

You may now proceed with your working. You may physically
walk to a tree that you would like to connect with, if you are not
there already, or you may sit down and perform the journey in
your mind. Whichever you decide, know that you are now between
the worlds.

Once you are at the tree that you wish to symbolise the World
Tree, take a moment and stand before it, honouring it. Ask for
permission to come closer, to share in its wisdom. If the answer
is yes, then proceed forward and touch the trunk of the tree. If
the answer is no, perhaps you will need to seek another tree, or
clarify your intention to the tree before you can receive a positive
response.

With your hands upon the bark, feel the power of the tree
flowing upwards from the earth, and also downwards from the
branches. Feel where it meets, and connect to that energy. You
can then visualise a doorway opening up in the trunk of the tree
beneath your hand, and with the slightest of movements it swings
open, revealing a staircase that travels downwards. You enter, and
proceed down the dimly lit stairwell, the roots of the tree all around
you, the smell of the earth clean and clear. The light brightens as
you descend, and eventually you reach the bottom of the stairs
and find yourself in a world very similar to that above ground,
only that there is no obvious source for the light; there is no sun
and moon, no stars, only a silver light that illuminates everything.
It is neither day nor night, and the season may be different to that
above. Take a moment and orient yourself to this new world. You
find that you are standing next to a tree of the same type you used
above ground to enter into the Lowerworld. You take your hand
and place it upon the trunk, and call to the Lowerworld to reveal
to you your spirit guide, whether in the form of an ancestor or that
of the Fair Folk.

A mist appears around you, and slowly clears revealing a figure standing before you. You take a moment to look at the figure, and you incline your head towards it in a slight bow. You can ask the figure if they are to be your spirit guide in the Lowerworld. If the answer is yes, then you can proceed to ask them further questions, and get to know them. If the answer is no, then you can ask them to direct you to your guides. One will appear.

Once you have met and spoken with your guide, you give your thanks and then return to the Middleworld. Place your hand once more upon the trunk of the tree, and a doorway appears. You travel up the stairwell back the way you came. The light of the Lowerworld recedes behind you as another light beckons you back towards the Middleworld. You step out from the doorway into the Middleworld, and the doorway closes and vanishes back into the tree. You say a prayer of thanks to the World Tree, and then return back to your original starting point.

Once at your starting point, say these or similar words:

I now return from walking between the worlds.
I honour my time spent in the Lowerworld
And seek to bring its wisdom into my being.
May I walk the realms in beauty and in truth
And may my eyes be open to the possibilities.
I honour my spirit guide and my work.
May I be the awen.

Turn three times clockwise and state:

By the power of three times three
This is my will, so may it be.

Take a moment to settle back into this world. If you can, eat and drink something to ground you in the present moment. You might clap your hands three times, or pat the earth three times to signal your full return. You can also say your name aloud three times. Journal your experience as soon as you are able.

Chapter Eight

The Middleworld (Abred)

The Middleworld is the place where we live most of our lives. Yet it is not "ordinary" or dull in any sense in comparison to the other worlds. The Middleworld is a place where the worlds of Upper and Lower come together and dance right before our very eyes. It can be a wondrous hill in the middle of a plain that we can visit, walk up, sit on and meditate. It can be a deep well that bubbles to the surface where the sunlight sparkles upon it. It can also be the trunk of a tree in our own backyard, where we can travel up and down to the lower and upper worlds respectively.

The Middleworld, as the place where we spend most of our time, requires us to be fully awake to it, to establish a deep and intimate relationship with it. We need to know the land upon which we live, where we make our homes and walk the dogs. We need to know the names of the trees and plants, the geological formations, the rivers and streams and where they run. Through a practice of deep connection, we work with the Middleworld and realise that it's just as wondrous as the Lower or Upper worlds of Annwn and Gwynfed.

In the tree motif, the Middleworld is the trunk, the strong and sturdy part of the tree that connects the Lower and Upper worlds. If you have found a connection with a particular tree, perhaps in your garden or local park, forest or woodland, then you can use this tree easily for connecting the three worlds of Lower, Middle and Upper. Simply by leaning your back onto the trunk of the tree, you can connect with it and open your awareness to the present moment, the Middle world, with ease.

Connecting to the Middle World

The Hedge Druid sits with her back against the trunk of a great

tree, in between all the worlds. Spending most of her time in the
Middleworld, when she works with the Hedge Druid's Craft she
can also use the tree to travel to the lower and upper worlds. From
the centre spreads the Middleworld. It is the centre, the central axis
of the Wheel of the Year. It is the circle's centre, the stillness of the
centre, from which radiates all life. When we return to the centre

we return to ourselves, and to the heart of the cosmos. We see that the universe is reflected in the tree, and also within ourselves. We understand, truly understand how much we are a part of each other. We are the universe, the cosmos, and the cosmos is us.

In an eighth-century Irish text we find the hero, Finn mac Cumhall encountering a man sitting in a tree. This could very well be the World Tree, a connecting motif that binds Celtic mythology to a host of other world religions, and which holds the tree as a gateway to between the worlds. The sacred *bile* of the Celts was a totem for their tribe, a central axis for their everyday life.

In this particular story of Finn mac Cumhall, the man in the tree has the blackbird at his right shoulder, a stag at the foot of the tree and a vessel of white bronze in his left hand with some water and a fish, most likely a salmon, though some have translated the fish as a trout. The figure in the tree was cracking hazelnuts, the food that provided divine wisdom, that in other tales falls into the pool where the salmon swim, making them some of the wisest creatures on earth. The man gives half of a hazelnut to the blackbird, and eats the other half himself. From the depths of the water-filled vessel, he takes an apple, another symbol of the Otherworld, and gives half to the stag and eats the other half himself. He then drinks from the vessel and offers it to all other three animals.

In this tale, we can surmise that the salmon represents the Lowerworld, the stag the Middleworld and the blackbird the Upperworld. The man in the tree connects them all, being in and working in the Middleworld. The importance of trees to the Celts cannot be understated. Using the tree as a motif to travel between the worlds can be of great benefit in the Hedge Druid's Craft, connecting us to our ancient past. One thing you can do is to look into the history and mythology of the Celts in relation to the blackbird, the stag and the salmon. If you find one of these becomes your totem animal, take an even deeper look armed with the knowledge of Finn mac Cumhall's encounter with the man in the tree. Use the tree that you work with on the physical plane, and with its permission, learn all that you can from that experience.

The Middleworld is that which connects the Lowerworld and the Upperworld to our present moment, to our everyday life. It is the trunk of the tree, between the lower and upper worlds. It is stable and supportive. It is that part that we can physically touch, connect with. It is right here, right now, right in front of us.

The spirits of nature are all around us, existing in this present moment, alongside us in the Middleworld. These are the spirits of "now": of the sun shining on our faces, the rain beating upon the windows, the tremor of the earthquake, the rushing of the river, the running of the deer. It is the world of spirit made manifest. It is atoms buzzing along creating mass and density out of seeming nothingness. It is tangible and right in front of our noses. It is inspiring and beautiful, horrific and fearsome. It is all that is happening in this present moment, and all who share this point in life with us at this particular time. It is myriad stories coming together in a shared reality.

The Middleworld is also a liminal place, a place where two things come together. It is where the shore meets the sea, where the land meets the sky, where the bubbling spring comes out of the ground. It is a place that requires us to pay attention, to listen to the wisdom that is flowing around us each and every second. It teaches us the importance of listening, and of being present. If we don't pay attention, the Middleworld passes us by.

And so we work diligently with the Middleworld. We come to know our home environments. We study and learn the names of plants and animals that live around us in our own locality. We learn where our water comes from. We learn how to work with the Middleworld in deep, sustainable relationship. We learn our place in the Middleworld, our functioning part of the ecosystem. We must maintain the practice of deep connection in the Middleworld, mundane though it may appear to be at times. When we have the thread of connection running through our lives, nothing is ever mundane, and all is sacred.

We must learn to be good neighbours. "Good neighbours" was once a term used for the Sidhe, for the Faerie or Fair folk. We can use this term to apply to ourselves as well, in learning about our relationship with the world. It can't be a one-sided thing. We once left out offerings to these folk: cream and butter, or items of great worth such as swords and torcs offered into lakes and bogs. We can work once again to establish a relationship with the world around us and its legion of beings through the making of offerings, each and every day, once a week, once a month. The amount of offerings is not important, it's the intention behind them and the consistency with which you work in your own life that is of utmost importance.

We do the research, and we learn about where we live. We then give back, in gratitude for our many blessings. We may leave food out for local wildlife or for the Fair Folk every Monday, or after a ritual at the full or new moon. We might once a month sacrifice a day of our weekend to do a litter pick-up, or work at a homeless shelter. We might stuff envelopes for an environmental or animal charity. We give back, working with reciprocity.

If we look back to the tree, the tree is a magnificent creation of life. It is a manifestation of divine energy. It is spirit made matter. It is utterly inspiring. It gives and it gives, working with its environment to the best of its ability. We, in the Hedge Druid's Craft, can be like the oak. We have to use our time in the Middleworld to connect to this energy. Go out and try to find an oak tree. Lay your hand upon the bark and think about all that an oak does for us and for the environment.

For instance, a large oak tree (around 200-300 years old) will provide enough oxygen for one human for an entire year. It takes a dangerous gas, carbon dioxide, and uses it as fuel to feed itself, in turn producing oxygen as a by-product of its consumption. If only we could be so kind in our own consumption! An oak tree is also very sturdy; its root system stretches as far below the ground as does its canopy reach towards to sky. These roots are constantly changing as well; when food, water and other nutrients have been depleted in a particular area, the roots die off, and new ones grow in other areas, stretching out and reaching for potential food sources. These roots work in close combination with mycorrhizal fungi, tiny thin strips of filament-like spider's webs, to break down substances as hard as stones and reach the nutrients within. These mycorrhizal fungi also act as great communication networks beneath forest and plants, keeping everything in contact with each other. It is a symbiotic relationship; once could not exist without the other. We need to relearn the importance of such relationships, for we are symbiotic with trees.

We might also take our inspiration from the animal kingdom around us, and in doing so find our animal guides to help us in the Middleworld. There will be more on finding your animal guide in a later chapter.

You can perform a ritual similar to that which you undertook into the Lowerworld, but *remain* in the Middleworld. Seek out your guides, the spirits of place and of nature all around you here in the Middleworld, perhaps meeting them outside the trunk of the World Tree. Let them inspire you to find your place in your environment, and to guide you in your work.

Chapter Nine

The Upperworld (Gwynfed)

This is the realm of inspiration, where immortal beings dwell, The Shining Ones. It's a place of divine beings and teachers of tradition. It is the place where the spark that begins the intention is formed, to come into manifestation. It is the waving boughs of the world tree, reaching towards the heavens, yet connected to the deep earth through the trunk, rooted into the soil as it reaches for the stars.

The Upperworld is a place of light, but this is not the sort of good/ evil connotation that usually abounds in modern thinking, where darkness is evil and light is good. The darkness of the Lowerworld is the darkness of mystery and transformation, the lightness of the Upperworld is that of illumination and enlightenment. We need both in our lives, and cannot ignore one or the other. The Upperworld is often called the realm of the gods, but this too is an over-generalisation. The gods exist in all three worlds. The Upperworld is perhaps the place of form, where the "purest" form or archetypes can be found for many.

In the Hedge Druid's Craft we work with the Upperworld after becoming familiar with the Lowerworld and Middleworld, first. We need the knowledge and stability from these planes of existence before we move up into the branches of the world tree, otherwise our foundation is shaky and we can easily topple over in the slightest of breezes. We need to know who we are, through our ancestors, and where we are, in the present moment, before we pursue the greater mysteries and questions of humanity and our own souls.

Connecting to the Upperworld

In those lofty realms of the sacred *bile*, the world tree of the Celts, is the realm where the gods are said to dwell. It is often said that the ancestors belong to the Underworld, we are in the Middleworld, and the gods reside in the Upperworld. Of course, we know that all beings can move about from one world to the other, and often do, using those liminal times and passages, using ritual or their own innate power to move from one realm to the next. In the Hedge Druid's Craft, we learn the techniques for doing so, through journeying, through herb, plant and animal lore, through ritual, spells and charms.

The Upperworld is often seen as reaching the highest spiritual state. When we travel there, we open our awareness to The Big Picture, to the grander overall patterns of the universe. Here, we don't deal with the trivial matters; this is the place where we find deep integral wisdom, where we learn the lessons of the universe in total, utter being. It is a state of grace, one reached often through ecstatic ritual. It is the place of wisdom, knowledge and prophecy. It is the realm of the celestial heavens, the stars, sun and moon.

When we view the tree of life as our very own being, the roots are our roots, reaching deep into the soul, grounding us, allowing us access to the ancestors, to our blood roots, to the land. The trunk is our body in the here and now, interacting with everything, and with all the worlds. The branches are our consciousness, reaching ever higher. We often hear this equated with the realm of spirit.

Reaching out our own consciousness towards the Upperworld, we expand our souls. We come to the realisation that everything is energy. We learn the lessons of transformation, of integration, of wholeness. Rooted in our previous work, and awake to the present moment, we move towards a state that is not a state, into utter immersion with the universe. A word that is often used is transcendence. It is the place of the Higher Self, of the soul in its purity, untainted by shadow.

Often the Upperworld is equated with the destination of the soul's journey. It is the ultimate truth. It is also the place of the future. With our minds, we create the present and map the future.

That future exists in the Upperworld, waiting for our intention to bring it into manifestation. The Upperworld is also the place of creativity.

Working with the Upperworld, we can literally change our lives. It is a place to change perception, for from our higher vantage point we may be able to see that what we thought was true was only part of the truth. We can look deeply and honestly at all aspects of ourselves and our work, and see the reality and the truth behind the veils of illusion that we create. We see through expectations and false perceptions. We are like the hawk, circling on high, seeing all below with a detached mind and then choosing to strike where and when we see fit. In the Upperworld, we ride the winds of change.

We live our lives with perceived, immutable truths. Most of these are simply opinions that we have repeated back to ourselves over and over again until we made them a truth. When we work with the Upperworld, we see that we are all simply stories, and no story holds an immutable truth. Every story has perceptions, perspectives. When we look beyond these, then we begin to see the overarching pattern of being, which is not beholden to any perspective.

We must gain a clarity of vision, releasing shadow perspectives in order to see the world anew. With fresh eyes and a new perspective, we can change ourselves. In changing ourselves, we can begin to change the world. We can use our guides which we have met in the Lower and Middleworld, to help us find this new perspective, and then perhaps to let go of all perspectives entirely and just be. Though we all work through the lens of our own perception, we can become aware of this lens, and work to see beyond it as much as we possibly can.

We have the ability to create and change our worlds to some extent. Yes, there are overriding factors in everyone's lives that have a bearing upon what it is that we are able to do. However, our perception is something that is entirely under our control, if we have learned to work with our shadow aspect (that which is "hidden" or unconscious) and have received guidance from our teachers and guides in this realm and in the Otherworld.

We've heard the term "the sky's the limit". Here we see resonance with the Upperworld. We may carry a vision of who it is that we wish to be, and that image resides in the Upperworld. It is up to us to manifest that here and now, in the present moment. Otherwise, it will live forever just out of reach. It requires hard work and dedication. It requires us to look deeply at ourselves, and to move beyond outdated and outmoded patterns of behaviour. It requires us to want to change.

When creating a rite to enter into the Upperworld, we might beforehand research the local gods of our area, to see if we can find their names, such as Andraste of the Iceni tribe near to where I live. We might come up with our own names for the gods of our local deities of valley and hillside, of the city or the seaside town after having spent much time reaching out towards them, if their names cannot be found, or they might also wish to remain unnamed. What matters most is that we make the effort to know the gods of these places, so that we can deepen our relationship to the land and in doing so, better serve it in our Druidry.

To enter into the Upperworld, go to your special, liminal place where you begin all your hedge riding work. Assume the Druidic pose, the one-legged "within this world and the other" posture described previously, or simply place your non-dominant foot forward. When you are ready, say the following or similar words:

I walk between the worlds with the World Tree as my guide;
May my roots reach deep,
May my core be strong and centred, and
May my inspiration reach towards the skies.
I now venture into the Upperworld
To understand my highest potential,
To seek the inspiration to guide me,

And to connect with the Shining Ones (or gods).
In the realms above I seek my divine truth
To bring it back into the Middleworld.
May I be aided in this endeavour
By those who are attuned with my intention.

Turn around counter-clockwise three times, and then state:

By the power of three times three,
This is my will, so may it be.

You can now proceed with your working, knowing that you are now between the worlds. Go to the World Tree, and open the doorway to the Upperworld as you did with the Lowerworld. When a doorway appears, you see a staircase leading up, and slowly you begin to climb, following the light that is neither daylight nor starlight. Take a moment and orient yourself to this new world. You take your hand and place it upon the trunk, and call to the Upperworld to reveal to you your guide in the Upperworld, whether that be the gods or the Fair Folk of the Upperworld (The Shining Ones).

A mist appears around you, and slowly clears revealing a figure standing before you. You take a moment to look at the figure, and bow deeply towards it. You can ask the figure if they are to be your spirit guide in the Upperworld, and whether they are from the realm of the gods or the Shining Ones. If the answer is yes, then you can proceed to ask them further questions, and get to know them. If the answer is no, then you can ask them to direct you to your guides. One will appear.

Once you have met and spoken with your guide, you give your thanks and then return to the Middleworld. Place your hand once more upon the trunk of the tree, and a doorway appears. You travel down the stairwell back the way you came, the light of the Upperworld receding behind you as another light beckons you back towards the Middleworld. You step out from the doorway into the Middleworld, and the doorway closes and vanishes back into the tree. You say a prayer of thanks to the World Tree, and then return back to your original starting point.

Once at your starting point, say these or similar words:

I now return from walking between the worlds.
I honour my time spent in the Upperworld
And seek to bring its wisdom into my being.
May I walk the realms in beauty and in truth
And may my eyes be open to the possibilities.
I honour the gods (or Shining Ones) and my work.
May I be the awen.

Turn three times clockwise and state:

By the power of three times three
This is my will, so may it be.

Take a moment to settle back into this world. If you can, eat and drink something to ground you in the present moment. You might clap your hands three times, or pat the earth three times to signal your full return. You can also say your name loud three times. Journal your experience as soon as you are able.

Working with religion, spirituality and philosophy will unalterably change your life. I hope that walking the path of the Hedge Druid's Craft, riding the hedge and working with the World Tree will have meaning for you and that you will be able to see and achieve that vision of yourself which you wish to achieve in this lifetime. Moving through outmoded perspectives, we can change the pattern of our lives for the better. Working with the Upperworld does just that. We recognise the patterns when we work with the Lowerworld. In the Middleworld, we change our behaviour in order to change the pattern. And the end result of working with all the worlds is that we become the pattern of the universe itself.

I hold a vision of myself that is linked to the Upperworld. This vision of my self is untainted by shadow aspects. I work with the Lowerworld to uncover the shadow aspects of myself, and in the Middleworld change my behaviour and my life in order to release these patterns of behaviour that are holding me back from achieving my vision, the Hedge Druid's Craft that I wish to follow. That vision is mine alone, holding my highest aspirations for myself and the world. In reaching out toward it, from the highest branches of the world tree, I stretch myself beyond my own seeming capabilities, and letting go I am able to touch and become that vision. I am connected to that vision of myself through the tree, rooted deep and stretching tall, allowing all three worlds to move through me, to nourish and sustain me.

Part Three

Lore

Chapter Ten

Plant Lore

Anyone worth their salt working with the Hedge Druid's Craft has got to know at least *something* about the local flora. To access the realm of plants means that we must come into good relationship with them. We begin to see the interdependence that we have on plants, the fact that we could not survive without them. The very fact that plants give off oxygen which we need to breathe, and take in the carbon dioxide that we exhale shows the very fundamental nature of this relationship, of give and take. The Hedge Witch, the Wise Woman, or the Druid would have a working knowledge of the plants in her area, their physical and spiritual/magical uses. Here I will go through a few of the plants in my local area in the East of England, which I work with, to give you an idea of how we can work with the realm of plants as a Hedge Druid.

Sometimes charms were used when picking and harvesting a plant. Alexander Carmichael's *Carmina Gadelica* published in the early twentieth century is full of country wisdom gleaned and recorded for posterity. Many of the charms and blessings in this six-part work are obviously of Pagan origin, and have been adapted for use by Christians. There are many examples of charms to be said for picking various herbs, and I would recommend taking a look at this material, as well as Morgan Daimler's book *By Land Sea and Sky*, wherein she offers a re-Paganised version of the text. Always remember to give back for what you take: say a prayer of thanks, bury a penny in the soil, or give an offering of milk or honey to the plant. Also, never take so much that the plant will not recover. If you require the root, ensure that other plants are growing nearby. If it is the only plant in the area, leave it alone. Grow your own if you can. Note that harvesting and collecting many wild plants in Britain have strict laws surrounding them.

Plants growing near roadsides may be too polluted to use; allow common sense to guide you.

Before you begin working with any plants, you must know exactly what species you are working with, whether it is poisonous or not, edible or inedible. Some plants will be contraindicative with certain medications, and so once again you must consult a qualified herbalist or medical doctor before ingesting any herbs. Some are poisonous merely through contact with the skin, and so when picking herbs you absolutely must know what you are doing. There are several plants and fungi here in the British Isles that are deadly; do not become a statistic.

Here are the three plants that I work with the most, in full detail:

NETTLE (Urtica Dioica); Plant Family: (Hamamelids)

Parts Used: Leaves, buds, rhizomes and roots.

Collection season: early spring for leaves and buds until they flower, seeds and roots in autumn.

Soil and Environment: Universal throughout British Isles and most of temperate world, found in forests, woods, river banks, under shrubs and bushes, wasteland – pretty much anywhere. Thrives in nitrogen-rich soil.

Propagation: Wind-pollinated perennial.

Description: Up to 5ft tall, with long jagged edge to shield-shape leaf that comes to point at tip. Stinging hairs along leaves and square stalks. Small, creamy-green flowers in long strands, seeds not long after flowering.

History: A sacred herb to the Anglo-Saxons (wergulu) and used in medieval times as beer to treat rheumatism. Tibetans believe their sage and poet, Milarep (CE 1052-1135) lived on nettle soup until he turned green. Nettle tops were used as a rennet substitute in cheese-making as they turned milk sour. There are around 500 species of nettle.

Chemical constituents: Chlorophyll, vitamins A, B complex, C, D, E and K, folic acid, minerals, bioflavinoids, seretonin precursor.

Actions and Medicinal Uses: Reduces fatigue, improves stamina, nourishes kidneys, adrenal glands, nourishes immune, digestive, endocrine and respiratory system, increases metabolism, normalises weight, eases/prevents rheumatism and arthritis, good for skin and hair, eases lung complaints such as asthma. Galactagogue. Eases leg cramps and muscle spasms. Reduces haemorrhoids. Anti-inflammatory, alterative, astringent, haemostatic, circulatory tonic, diurectic.

Combinations: Can be used to "boost" many other herb actions, especially when dealing with immune system.

Usage: Tea – 2 tsps steeped (dried) or 3 tsps (fresh) in 1 cup of boiled water for 5 to 10 mins three times a day. Tincture is 1 tsp twice a day.

Contraindications: None.

Spiritual Aspects: Protection, self-respect, resiliency and flexibility. Teaches healthy boundaries while providing deep nourishment. Good meditational tea and also cleansing/purifying bath before ritual.

Nettle is a wonderful herb for the Hedge Druid's Craft. Its prickly leaves and stem teach us of boundaries and respect. It grows abundantly almost anywhere, and it is brilliant for our health. A common "weed" found in hedges and roadsides, this understated plant was a staple for our ancestors. In the spring months, when food was scarce, it was nettle that was the first of the green to be seen, and it's nutrient-rich properties kept many a person alive until other food became available. Drink nettle tea to become stronger physically, mentally and spiritually.

BIRCH (Betula Pedula)

Plant family: Birch Family (Hamamelids)

Parts Used: Sap, leaves, bark and buds.

Soil and Environment: Woodland and heath, moor, parklands and gardens. Copes well in sandy, acidic soil and can handle being near the coast (salt). Native to northern temperate regions as it handles the cold well. Propagation by wind.

Description: Deciduous leaves, shield-shaped with jagged edges. White papery bark with horizontal darker stripes and marks. Base of trunk expanded where it meets the ground, compared to the slim rest of the trunk. Male and female catkins – male catkins produce a lot of pollen and cause many allergic reactions. Light "green" smell, leaves and bark taste bitter, sap is sweet. High energy, "talkative" tree.

History: Used for thousands of years in cold, northern climates in everything from adhesives to wine, baskets, yokes, boats and vinegar. Pioneer species when ice caps retreated 10,000 years ago, growing quickly and falling as it is a soft wood, then fertilizing the ground for other tree species. First letter of Ogham (Druid) alphabet. One of seven peasant trees in Brehon law. Birch was used throughout Europe at Winter Solstice or New Years to "beat the bounds". Bride's doll held a birch wand. Entire birch trees were offered in votive pits in ancient times. Twigs used for brooms (besoms). Considered the World Tree in many cultures (alongside Ash and Oak).

Chemical constituents: Birch camphor, tannins, triterpine (betulin), flavinoids, saponines, essential oils, mineral salts (calcium oxalate) vitamin C, aromatic hydrocarbons, sucrose. Rich in potassium. Birch sap contains betulinic acid, an anti-tumour cancer treatment.

Actions and Medicinal Uses: Birch sap is good for kidney or bladder stones, skin conditions and rheumatic diseases. It is also a good spring cleansing tonic and nutritive. Fermented it makes a lovely wine. Leaves and leaf buds good as tea for general detox, urinary complaints, cystitis, rheumatic and arthritic conditions, gout. Good diuretic. Astringent qualities and diuretic properties help with skin problems, sore throats and chest congestion when used as inhalation therapy. Effective germicide. Buds can be eaten for stomach complaints. Insect repellent.

Combinations it can be used in: Use with sodium bicarbonate

to improve tea's ability to cut through high uric acid levels. Oil and tea combine well together.

Usage: Birch sap tapped straight from tree and drunk as cleansing tonic. Tea to spring cleanse internally, as well as for gout, kidney and bladder stones, cystitis, arthritis, rheumatism, psoriasis, eczema, fluid retention and fevers. Birch leaf oil for topical use for cellulite, detox massage, aching muscles, rheumatism and arthritis, eczema and psoriasis, fibromyalgia.

Dosage: Tea – 4 to 5 leaves per cup or mug of boiling water, steeped for 5 to 10 minutes, taken 3 to 4 times per day. Sap – 3 tbsps in morning. Oil – use for massage as needed.

Contraindications: None.

Spiritual Aspects: New beginnings, adventure, feminine energy, creativity. Leading on with shining light through the dark forest of the soul. Brings hope and courage to discouraging situations. Aids in clear thinking and provides clarity of purpose. Encourages self-discipline and inner authority. Offering of birch wreaths can be made to water spirits to avoid storms or excessive rain. Good cleansing/purifying bath before ritual or mediation.

Birch twigs were traditionally used to make the bottoms of brooms that witches used, both for cleaning their homes and travelling between the worlds. These trees grow almost anywhere in Britain, and have a light, communicative energy. I've always found that birch trees are willing to talk to you, if you stop and take a moment to honour them. They can make excellent companions walking between the worlds.

OAK (Quercus robur)

Plant family: Beech family (fagaceae)

Parts Used: Bark, leaves, acorns, galls ("oak apples" created by gall wasps on leaves and also acorn or knopper gall, on acorn).

Soil and Environment: Hedgerows, woods, parkland. Copes well in moist and even poor soil. Interbreeds with other oak, such as sessile and downy oak. Grows very slowly.

Description: 130ft-160ft (40m-50m). Lives between 400-1,000 years. Circumference to approximately 30ft (10m). Lobed leaves in ovoid shape. Scaled grey/green trunk with warty branches, scaly "capped" acorns longer than American cousin. Male flowers in yellow-green catkins, female flowers unassuming – both flowers grow on same tree. Due to size, creates a greenish light around it when found in a forest, as it opens up the canopy around it to let light in. Quiet tree, noble stillness, grand presence. Irregular-shaped crown with branches starting low down on trunk. Galls are smooth, globular, brown and perforated. Acorn or Knopper gall wasp (Andricus quercuscalicis) became established in the UK during the 1970s and is now widespread. Eggs are laid during early summer in the developing acorns of *Quercus robur*. Instead of the normal cup and nut, the acorn is converted into a ridged woody structure in which the gall wasp larva develops. The gall is initially yellowish-green and sticky but later comes greyish brown. The next generation of wasp forms inconspicuous galls on the male catkins of Turkey oak, *Quercus cerris* the following year, rotating each year between the two tree species. Wasps know the concept of sustainability!

History: Used for building homes, ships, furniture, etc. Bark used in tanning leather and dyeing fabric. Acorns used to feed pigs (and humans when food was scarce). Galls used to make ink. The wood is good for burning and for making charcoal. Oak trees have sheltered many famous outlaws, including Robin Hood and Charles II. Oak is the second Ogham in the aicme of Huath. Oak forests covered most of Europe in vast expanses. It is one of the seven "nobles of the wood" in Brehon law. Associated in Celtic lore with thunder and lightning, oak trees often survive lightning strikes. Their roots reach as deep into the ground as their branches reach high into the sky. Oak was the first tree species to be protected by legislation. It is the chieftain tree of the Druids: Druid means "wisdom of the oak". The Oak King battles the Holly King at each solstice; The Oak King is the god of summer. Lightning-struck oak trees were important in Druid and Celtic magic. Sacred to the goddess Brighid, her original sanctuary in Kildare was a grove of oak trees: Cill Dara, the church of the oak tree. In Greece the rustling of the leaves and branches was used for divination. Woodhenges of Neolithic or Bronze Age were made of oak, such as Seahenge in Norfolk. Sometimes considered the World Tree in certain cultures, it was an *axis mundi*. Neolithic trackways of oak still exist in Britain. Oak used to be on sixpences and shillings. King Arthur's table at Winchester is cut from a single piece of oak tree trunk.

Chemical constituents: Tannins, tanning acids, minerals.

Actions and Medicinal Uses: Astringent and good for tightening, drying, binding and toning tissue, reducing excess discharge. Good for diarrhoea, dysentery, eye, mouth and throat inflammations as well as inflammation in the mucous membranes of the digestive tract. Good for burns, sores, bleeding. Also, good for coughs and colds. Anti-microbial and anti-septic. Good for sweaty feet, chilblains and anal tears (taken as bark decoction in room temperature bath). Acorn coffee aids poor digestion. Used homoeopathically for alcoholism. Helps reduce fever. Beneficial hair rinse for dandruff and hair loss. Compresses soaked in tea can shrink goitres and glandular inflammation. Anti-inflammatory.

Combinations: Oak bark decoction with nettle and yarrow make a good women's tonic. Bruised leaves when applied with comfrey leaves help heal bruises and sprains.

Usage: Leaves for tea and tincture, bark as decoction, acorns ground and roasted for coffee substitute. Tea and decoction internal use: 2 tsps dried or 3 tsps fresh leaf/bark per cup of boiled water up to 3 times per day. Tincture: 1 tsp three times per day. Leaf galls as tincture internally for severe diarrhoea and dysentery. Use decoction as local astringent externally for haemorrhoids. Bruised leaves for first aid treatment in bruises, swelling and sprains.

Contraindications: Possible contraindication when used with morphine. Possible antagonist to nicotine sensitivity.

Spiritual Aspects: Oak is sacred to many gods. The Proto-Indo-European word for oak, *dorw*, became the word for "door". Oak is a doorway between the worlds, as it lives between the worlds (high branches, deep roots). Celtic priests ate acorns to aid in powers of divination. Oak was popular in the funeral ceremonies of ancient Celts. Acorns kept in the home or carried on a person bring good luck. Oak teaches us about strength, even when the worst happens (as they often survive lightning strikes). For Druids, they symbolise the ideal way of life, with branches reaching towards the heavens while feet are rooted deeply in the earth. Water found in the tree's nooks and crannies can provide a good vibrational essence for empowerment, fighting great difficulties, loss of hope or the draining of energy. Oak helps develop inner sovereignty. It leads to greater ability for kindness and compassion. Promotes personal responsibility. Spirit ally to connect you with other worlds. Oak is the doorway to new worlds and new perception.

Oak is a wonderful ally in the Hedge Druid's Craft. As the oak tree's roots extend as far down into the soil as the boughs reach overhead, it is in the perfect balance between the worlds. Some oak trees in Britain are hundreds, if not over one thousand years old. They can be great teachers, but some can be very impatient with humanity, and want nothing to do with us. We must respect this.

Other plants which I work with are:

Plantain (Plantago lanceolota) – leaf

- Antihistamine – good for insect bites, hay fever tea
- vulnerary (wound healer) used as a poultice for clearing heat and inflammation, varicose veins and varicose eczema
- purifying quality – used as a poultice to draw out dirt from wounds
- relieves toothache and inflammation in gums
- soothes mucous membranes of digestive tract – good for stomach ulcers and IBS, useful in healing and strengthening

digestive system
- expectorant – useful for stubborn coughs and chronic bronchitis, also good for dry coughs
- greater plantain (hoary or major as otherwise known) good for relieving tired feet

Used as tea, tincture and succus, as well as for poulticing.
*Note: only anti-bacterial when used fresh.

Chickweed (Stellaria media) – aerial parts

- skin soother, with cooling, drawing action when applied to bites, stings and rashes (can be used straight from picking or crushed first), helps to clear eczema, rheumatic joint conditions and varicose veins
- soothes internal organs as well due to high level of saponins, which help organ membranes to absorb nutrients better – used for gastritis, colitis, congested chest, blocked kidneys and gallbladder, lungs, sore throats and bronchitis
- excellent spring tonic – high levels of vitamin A and C, as well as iron, copper, calcium and magnesium – juice or eat fresh in salads
- slimming aid – stimulates urine, high saponin levels help to dissolve fat

Used as tea, eaten fresh in salads or pesto, as a bath oil or vinegar, applied to rashes, stings and bites.

Elder (Sambuccus nigra) – flowers and berries

- febrifuge – used to break fevers (blossom)
- flowers support circulation (lymphatic system), promotes elimination through urinary tract, cuts congestion and inflammation of upper-respiratory tract, breaks up catarrh

- reduces symptoms of hay fever, often used with nettle in this instance
- berries reduce the length and severity of colds and flu, also good for coughs
- flowers and berries are anti-viral

Used as tea, tincture, glycerite or succus, cordial or syrup.

Hawthorn (Crataegus oxycanthus) – leaf, blossom and berry

- Hawthorn is a good heart tonic, beta blocker, protects the heart muscle, prevents heart attacks, is a vaso-dilator (peripheral), helps promote sleep and is the best herb for blood circulation
- regulates low blood pressure, steadies the heartbeat and lowers cholesterol. It contains chemical compounds that keep blood vessels open, and it vital where vessels lack tone and are inert due to fatty or calcium deposits
- lessens pain in the heart and adjacent areas, re-elasticates blood vessel walls (through rutin), rebuilds collagen fibres in outer layers of vessels and is a powerful anti-oxidant, as well as being rich in vitamin C
- reduces inflammation, relaxes the smooth muscles of the uterus, intestines and other areas to relieve congestion and reduces water retention (bloating before period)
- also aids digestion and eases sore throats

This herb is to be used as a tea, syrup (berries) and as a tincture.

*Not to be used with other beta-blockers or heart drugs/herbs. Please consult a qualified herbalist if on heart/blood pressure medication of any kind.

Meadowsweet (Filipendula ulmaria) – flowers

- analgesic, antispasmodic, anti-inflammatory and anti-rheumatic (good for arthritis sufferers
- thins the blood, is astringent and also works as a diuretic
- balances stomach acid as is good for treating diarrhoea, and is also good for treating colds and flu, headaches and reduces fever
- excellent pain reliever and is also good for cystitis and urethritis, breaking down kidney stones and gravel

This herb is used as a tea, tincture, glycerite and compress.

*There are contra-indications present, especially if you are on anti-coagulant medication such as for a stroke.

Motherwort (Leonorus Cardiaca) – herb *also known as *Lionheart*

- good heart tonic
- reduces blood pressure and lowers cholesterol, also reducing hardening of the arteries
- galactagogue and also a sedative
- It is anti-spasmodic and aids in nervous complaints
- It also reduces pain from angina pectoris. It helps treat migraines and panic attacks, and is good for menopause
- It helps correct anaemia, flatulence and diarrhoea

This herb is used as a tincture, tea or powder (capsule).

*There are contra-indications, especially with pregnant women.

Skullcap (Scutulleria nodosa) – herb

- Rebuilds myelin sheath (which helps to support and strengthen the nervous system)
- Nervine, anti-spasmodic, brain tonic, anodine,

anaphrodisiac
- Rich in B vitamins
- Good for anxiety, tension, panic attacks, muscle pain, menstrual pain, PMS
- Lifts depression, promotes sleep, relieves nervous exhaustion
- Good for addiction when coming off conventional pharmaceuticals such as anti-depressants
- Good for arthritis

This herb is used as a tea or tincture.

Dandelion (Taraxacum officinale) – root and leaf

- prime diuretic (providing potassium even as it releases excess water) as well as eliminates uric acid (good against gout and arthritis)
- bitter tonic (strengthens the liver)
- mild laxative
- kidney tonic and useful for treating liver conditions (introduce slowly as it increases bile)

This herb is used as a tea, tincture, decoction or the leaves eaten fresh in salads.

Heather (Calluna vulgaris) or (Erica cinerea "bell heather") – flowers

- antiseptic (good for treating wounds as a poultice)
- diuretic (flushes your system of toxins)
- disinfector for urinary tract
- increases urinary production
- diaphoretic (induces perspiration, so lowers body temperature and good for fevers)

- expectorant, anti-tussive (good for coughs)
- vasoconstrictor (good for low blood pressure)
- anti-arthritic, anti-rheumatic and sedative

As a tea or tincture, it is good to treat coughs and colds, also used to treat kidney and bladder stones, cystitis and inflammatory bladder conditions. Main uses are as cleansing and de-toxifying remedy, as well as being very helpful in treating rheumatism, arthritis, gout and metabolic conditions. Hot poultice used for chilblains.

These are just some of the plants which I work with in the Hedge Druid's Craft. Many of them such as nettles, chickweed and hawthorn, plantain and elder are found in hedgerows. There are many, many more that we can work with, and I have recommended some further reading at the end of this book. There are thousands of plants that we can work with in our practice, and many will hopefully relate to our local environment. Get to know your local plants, and if you live far away from anywhere where you can access the plant realm easily, then grow your own. All it takes is a windowsill and a pot, and you can grow many different herbs from seed which you can use in your work.

When we establish a relationship with the green and growing realm, we begin to understand and find our place in it. We need to understand how an ecosystem works, in order to live with it in balance and harmony. If we take too much, if we have too much of a harmful impact, then we must learn how to live differently. In working with the Hedge Druid's Craft, much like the work of the Wise Woman or Hedge Witch, we can find a sustainable relationship with the plant realm in order to both honour it and our own being. For one cannot exist without the other. We will look further at magical uses for certain herbs later in this book.

Chapter Eleven

Animal Lore

When working with The Hedge Druid's Craft we should hold a practical knowledge of the local fauna of the area. We know that animals are important allies in helping us to understand how we fit in the ecosystem. We know that the flights of birds can have meaning; that if the bees suddenly stop buzzing and hide that there is bad weather on the way. We know where the adder lives, and where the fallow deer give birth. We are a part of our environment, and all these animals and more are our neighbours, being just as important as our human neighbours for our community.

As I've previously mentioned, I live in horse country. These wonderful animals can teach us so much about co-operation. If we find a horse ally in our lives, then we learn about power and freedom, restraint and working together. I've lived around horses all my life, and not only are they an ally in the physical realm, but in the spiritual realm as well. I have a drum made out of pony skin (ethically sourced) which takes me on grand journeys to the Otherworld. A lot can be learned from working with horses both in the physical and in the astral, as they seem to teach us so much about ourselves and our own behaviour as well.

Cats have long been an animal ally to village Wise Women, the Cunning Folk and Witches. They have a long history of co-existence with humanity, and can be of great benefit. However, they can also have a huge impact on local wildlife, so if you've got a hunter cat and no barn to keep clear of mice, then you might want to consider belling the cat before she goes outside. Songbirds are especially on the decline due to cat predation, though humans are far worse! Some witches were believed to be able to shapeshift into a cat, and there are even superstitions that you shouldn't sleep with a cat in your room, for your soul becomes a moth at night and might get eaten up by a hungry feline! I have always lived with cats, and they have always slept with me at night, and I can vouch that my soul is completely intact each and every morning. My hair, which the cat has been sleeping on, is another matter, however...

Beekeeping is a country pursuit that is now slowly making its way into the suburbs of cities and towns. They were once referred to as "messengers of God" and needed to be kept up to date on the latest news. If there was a death in the family, you'd best tell the bees straight away, otherwise the hive might swarm or there might even be another death in the family soon. They were also told of happy events, such as weddings and births. By the way, folklore states that you should never swear near the hive; you might offend the bees.

Frogs and toads were often thought to be witches' familiars. They are a great asset to any gardener, and if you have the space you can create even the smallest of ponds where frogs can find shelter. Toads prefer to stay dry, so if you see a toad away from water, don't think that you are doing it a favour by placing it in the nearest pond. Both eat a host of insects that can be detrimental to your garden. Sadly, I no longer have any frogs in my garden, as the newts in the pond have taken over, and eat any and all frogspawn. However, the newts are just as lovely, and were considered witches' familiars as well.

Bats are marvellous creatures that help very much in keeping the mosquito population under control. The common pipistrelle can eat over three thousand insects in a single night. They are incredibly good to have around if you enjoy sitting in the garden late into the evening on a summer's night. Their flight and clicks from their sonar are very entertaining, and don't worry: they'll never get caught in your hair.

Owls are often associated with witches, and in the past had a bad press in Britain. However, times have changed, and now owls are regarded as some of the most popular birds in the country. There are five breeds: tawny, barn, little, short-eared and long-eared. Barn owls are my personal favourite, though their shriek is very eerie and unsettling. I have seen them many times while driving at dusk and at night, ghostly forms in the darkness. I even had one flying alongside my car for an entire length of a field – what a treat! In the back garden live tawny owls, whose calls can be heard all night long. They often accompany me in night-time rituals, and it is said that if an owl hoots as you finish casting a spell, it is doubly empowered.

The blackbird is sometimes known as the Druid dubh (the Black Druid). This is an important bird in the Hedge Druid's Craft, as blackbirds sing the most at the liminal times of dawn and dusk, in the twilight hours. They are often seen as messengers between the worlds. In the Welsh tale of *Culhwch and Olwen* the Blackbird of Cilgwri is one of the five oldest animals, which included The Eagle of Gwernabwy, the Stag of Rhedynfre, the Salmon of Glyn Llifon and the Owl of Cwm Cowlwyd. Blackbirds are also the allies of the goddess Rhiannon, who travel to the Otherworld of that Faerie Queen.

Some of the wild creatures can teach us a lot about living co-operatively. In my local area, we have the Silver-studded Blue butterfly. This butterfly, when in its caterpillar phase, secretes a substance which ants simply adore. These black ants take the caterpillar to their nest to keep it safe from predators, bringing it out to feed while keeping a close watch for any hungry birds or beasts nearby, much like a shepherd watching his flock. When the caterpillar turns into a chrysalis, it is still kept safe in the ants' nest, and emerges around eighteen days later, often still covered in their protective and adoptive ants (and uncles). They then fly on to seek the heather, where they will lay their eggs, which will turn into caterpillars once again to be reared by the ants. How amazing is that?

We also have nightjars in our area, and their distinctive *churring* sound can be heard in the deep twilight hours. Like the blackbird, it has huge eyes that help it to see in the dim light. These birds visit us in the summer all the way from Africa, flying across the Sahara Desert. They are very inquisitive birds, and will often fly around you to get a good look at you before they turn their attention back to hunting moths and other nocturnal insects. If you wear white, they will be doubly curious. Nightjars were often seen flying around cattle and sheep enclosures, and garnered the incorrect folk name of "goatsuckers", as they were believed to suck the animals' blood!

Sheep have long been reared in this part of the world, and are a large part of why the heathland exists in the first place. The original wild woodland that covered this entire island was cleared by Neolithic farmers. In this area of Suffolk in particular, areas were cleared and crops were grown for a season or two. The highly acidic and sandy soil soon lost all its nutrients, and so more woodland was cleared for new fields. What was left behind was then taken over by heather, which made for good grazing grounds for the nomadic shepherds thousands of years ago. Sheep have been a part of this landscape up until the last Sandlings shepherd retired, Mr Arthur Sutton, in the early 1970s. In the last few years some sheep have been brought back to graze and keep the heathland in shape, alongside the introduced Exmoor ponies. However, there is no "shepherd" per se that watches over them day and night, sleeping in a little shepherd's hut. You can still find the remains of a shepherd's cottage nearby, with his cottage garden grown wild, with damsons still appearing each autumn. Honouring the relationship between humans and animals in your local area can provide you with a rich sense of history and of place, where one can really feel a part of the landscape.

Some experiences that I've had with animals I'd like to share with you now, to demonstrate the incredible relationship that we can have with the natural world. Years ago now, I was hanging laundry outside and heard lots of shooting going on very close by. I decided to investigate, and walked down the bridleway to see what was going on. In the hedgerow two fields over, a group of men were shooting down crows. I can only assume that they were worried about their crop, but I had not ever seen a flock of crows in the area cause damage to crops; there is plentiful food in my area. However, sadly, lots of farmers and countryfolk simply shoot crows "for the fun of it", as there is no restriction on shooting these birds. I saw that they had already killed about twenty or thirty birds, as they lay dead or dying in the field. These were not birds that had been destroying a crop. They had shot a few down as they flew overhead, and as more crows came to see what was going on, these too were summarily shot. By the time I got there, there was a huge raucous in the skies as the crows screamed to their brethren below, trying to help their mates who had fallen. I have no doubt whatsoever that the crows were upset about what was happening, and not simply trying to feed on the recent carrion. Their cries were *different*, and it was being echoed throughout the whole landscape.

So there I stood, still on the bridleway, and saw what was going on. As crows came to investigate, cawing overhead to their friends fallen below, I waved my arms over my head and "shooed" them away. In my mind, I screamed *They have guns in the hedge, they will kill you!* The birds turned back at once, and began to relay the message to their friends. A few still came by, and I repeated my warnings, two or three more times, until no more crows came flying overhead. One of the men in the hedge came to the edge of bridleway and just looked at me, most likely wondering what in the world I was doing. I stood my ground, and soon all the men left, taking their guns with them. They left the carcasses of the crows in the field for a week. Not a single crow came to feast on the dead. The strange cries of the crows rang out across the village for days afterwards, mourning their loss. I prayed that evening in my garden for their strength, and a return to their numbers soon, and also for this to never happen again.

To this day, when I am out in my garden or wandering the heath, when a crow flies overhead it will usually "caw" at me once in a friendly greeting.

I have also had an extraordinary experience with a blue tit. I have always loved chickadees, having grown up in Canada and they being the equivalent of the little round birds here in the UK. A few years ago, I received the news that a friend of the family back in Canada had been murdered. We had known him for many, many years, and I had worked with him before I left home. When I received the dreadful news, I simply went into shock. I didn't know what to do, and there was so much I wanted to say to his family, to express my grief and condolences for their loss, but knew that a letter and card would possibly take weeks to reach them. Numbly I stood and walked to the window on the upper landing, and opened my heart in the hopes that they would be able to hear me, even though I was 3,000 miles away. At that moment, a blue tit flew up to the window and hovered just on the other side of the glass, eye-level with me. It seemed as though he was taking my message and, when I had finished, he flew off towards the west. I knew that my message was being delivered, and that magical moment helped to ease the pain and suffering. I also sent them that letter and card.

A more positive moment came to me as I was making my way across a little-used part of the heathland where I live. I stood by an old oak tree, which I spent a lot of time with, and meditated for a while before getting up and moving on. As I stood I saw across the small expanse the most beautiful pale stag. He was a fallow deer, with a rack that was enormous, so heavy that he had to hold his head in a certain regal position that made him all the more kingly. I had just asked for a blessing on the work that I was doing for Druid College, and then suddenly he appeared. He looked straight at me for many long minutes. Awestruck, I looked back, and a strange moment of being between the worlds passed as we gazed at each other, eye to eye. Finally, I remembered my manners, and bowed to him. He accepted my bow, and then I raised my staff high towards him. I could feel him bless the hazel staff, and as I brought it down by my side he nodded slightly, and then calmly and silently walked into the trees to disappear from sight.

Late one the summer I was in Tunstall Forest, on a lunch break and spending time in one of my favourite places: a birch wood. The leaves were starting to turn golden already, and I sat with my back against one of them, my eyes closed, listening to the song of the breeze through their leaves. I wanted to open my soul to new experiences and inspiration, and, well, the universe came through! All of a sudden I heard a rustling noise in the dry leaves of the forest floor, and turning to my right I saw about a dozen small snakes all winding their way towards me. I sat very still, and as they approached I saw that they were newly hatched adders (adders are the only snakes that are born "alive" and leave the nest straight away). Most of them simply flowed around me, intent on whatever journey awaited them on the heathland to my left. One came right up to me and sniffed the boot of my outstretched leg. I shifted ever so slightly so that it knew that I was not something to hide under, and it pulled back and slithered around me, re-joining its brothers and sisters on their trek towards the sun-drenched heath. It was an experience I shall never forget, and felt that I had been blessed as a Druid by one of the most sacred animals. (Adders were once a symbol of sun worship for the ancient Druids.)

These are only a few of the experiences that I have had with the animal world in my local area. I feel like I am a part of this ecosystem, and that we are all in this together. My lovely organic garden is a haven for pollinating insects and all manner of visitors from the other side of the hedge. I am truly blessed.

What follows is a ritual to help you find your animal ally. This might be in the spirit realm, in the physical, or both. It will help to bridge the worlds between human and non-human, teaching us to respect all of our neighbours and to work, live and learn together. You might find one or more animals that you can work with, either wild or domesticated. Pay attention to any animals that come across your path in the days following this ritual. They might be trying to communicate with you. Find out all that you can about

your animal ally, both in the spirit realm and in the flesh. Learning about their habitats, their behaviour and more can provide you with great insight into your own being.

Go to your liminal place, or the hedgerow. Assume the posture between the worlds, and then say the following words, or something similar:

I walk between the worlds, by the blessings of nature;
May I find deep and sustaining relationship with all manner of bird
*   and beast,*
The furred, feathered and finned, and
May I walk in spirit and in flesh with that which will guide me.
Come to me, great spirit;
Teach me of your ways.

I seek you out between the worlds
So that I may walk the path of the Hedge Druid's Craft
In all manner of wisdom.

Turn on the spot anti-clockwise three times, and say:

By the power of three times three
This is my will, so may it be

Proceed with your working/walking. Pay close attention to what you see and hear; you might not always see your spirit animal with your eyes, but it may call to you from a distance. Don't focus on only the "special" animals such as hawks or deer, but also look closely at the often ignored insects, snails, slugs, cows, sheep and other creatures that aren't quite as "sexy" as other totem animals are often portrayed. You may come across several creatures that have grabbed your attention, so make a mental note of them and, when you are finished, return to your original spot. Say the following words, or something similar:

I now return from walking between the worlds;
In harmony and in peace I return.
May my powers be strengthened,
May I receive protection in all my endeavours
As I work towards balance and harmony with the whole.
I honour my guides in the animal realm;
A blessing be upon them always and forever.

Turn clockwise three times, and state:

By the power of three times three
This is my will, so may it be.

Eat or drink something, clap your hands or say your name three times to return fully to this physical world. If you can, write down your experiences straight away so that you won't forget anything. Then start doing your research on what you have seen, and use that knowledge to help you build a strong relationship with the animal world, filled with wisdom and inspiration.

Chapter Twelve

Celestial and Weather Lore

The Celestial

The sun, moon and stars have equal importance in the Hedge Druid's Craft. With the cycles of the sun we find ourselves travelling through the year with agricultural festivals as well as the solstices and equinoxes being celebrated. The earth's orbit around the sun gives us our year, and its axis gives us our seasons. We can watch where the sun rises and sets each day, and make note in our own local area so that we will know that when the summer solstice arrives, the sun rising directly over the chimney of the pub, or behind a copse of trees on the hillside, or by the right-hand side of the neighbour's shed. Putting the great astronomical forces into the context of your local environment brings matters down to earth, if you'll pardon the pun.

There were 12-13 moons in each calendar year, and each had its own name that varied from region to region. This moon (which is where we get our term, "month") often relates to a natural phenomenon relevant to the time of year. Here is an example of each month's moon title, and if there are two full moons in a calendar month, the second is termed a "blue moon" (though this is historically incorrect, for a blue moon is actually the third full moon in an astronomical season with four full moons versus the normal three).

January – Wolf Moon
February – Snow Moon
March – Storm Moon
April – Growing Moon
May – Flower Moon
June – Mead Moon

July – Hay Moon
August – Corn Moon
September – Harvest Moon
October – Hunter's Moon
November – Frost Moon
December – Cold Moon

Two of these moons are especially noticeable because they rise on successive evenings more quickly than other moons. The Harvest Moon and Hunter's Moon have a shorter period of darkness between sunset and moonrise, and they both appear larger in the sky than any other moon. This is due to the Earth's tilt at that particular time of the year. These moons often appear very red in colour as they hang lower in the sky when viewed through the huge number of particles in the atmosphere.

Spend time watching where the moon rises and sets if you can. Notice how the arc of the moon's journey works in relation to the sun's journey in the sky and the seasons. Learn all that you can about how the phases of the moon are created, as well as those special times of both solar and lunar eclipses. During these moments, great works of magic can be performed, especially for the Hedge Druid's Craft, working as she does in those liminal times!

As well as the sun and moon, our work in the Hedge Druid's Craft should also consist of the knowledge of the stars in their whirling round each night. We can use the stars to navigate, or simply enjoy them, greeting them as old friends, some who are with us always, and some who only visit at certain times of the year.

You can locate the north celestial pole by finding the North Star, or Polaris as it is named. To do so, you must first find Ursa Major (in which you'll find smaller collections of star constellations such as the Plough which is sometimes called the Big Dipper). The Plough is easy to locate, made up of seven stars that form the shape of an old plough (before mechanised ploughs) or the shape of a ladle or "dipper". These stars are always visible in the northern hemisphere. At the lip of the cup furthest away from the handle, if you follow the line from the bottom to the top of the lip and extend that further, you will find that it points directly to Polaris. That is North.

You can use Polaris or any other star in magical workings, but note that not all stars are always in the sky all year round. Some of the brightest stars in the Northern hemisphere are:

Sirius
Alpha Centauri
Rigel
Belelgeuse
Aldebaran
Regulus

Find a good book on the starry heavens and learn what you can see from your area. If you live in a heavily populated area, only some of the brightest stars may be seen. If you are lucky enough to live in the countryside, you will have a much larger repertoire to work with. If you choose to do a magical working, or a hedge riding work at night, you can always connect to the energy of a chosen star first in order to boost your work. (You can do this during the day as well, but when the star is visible it has more impact on your psyche.) Before you begin your work, you might say something like:

Star of (name the star)
May your light shine upon me and my work.
May I join in your dance, as you dance the starry round.
Fill me with your light, neither of sun nor moon
But that of the silvery eldritch light of Faerie and the Otherworld.

Weather Lore

The local Wise Woman or Cunning Man would have a pretty good grasp on predicting the weather. So would local farmers, if they paid attention to their landscape, which, given it was their livelihood, I should imagine was the case! Get to know the weather patterns in your area, and make notes so that you can compare year upon year. Build up your own little system, as well as research meteorology. Here is some weather lore that applies to Britain which I use to help determine what is on its way.

Clouds are not only very pretty to look at, but can also tell us a great deal about what is happening in the skies, and what is to come. There are four types of clouds: stratus (layered), nimbus (rain clouds), cumulus (tall white or grey) and cirrus (very high and wispy). These form into three groups based on altitude and can help us predict the weather.

Low clouds are divided into:

- Cumulus: fluffy white clouds with rounded tops and flat bottoms. These usually indicate fair weather.
- Cumulonimbus: very tall, heaped clouds like grand castles in the sky. Light on the top and dark on the bottom. If you see one in the shape of an anvil, rain is definitely on the way. These clouds can indicate heavy rain and approaching thunderstorms, even hail.
- Stratus: low clouds that block out the sun or moon, either white or grey. In coastal areas or in hilly/mountainous regions, there can be a lot of rain.
- Stratocumulus: sometimes in grey sheets or like a large, lumpy grey pillow that covers the sky. To predict the weather with these, we need to look at which way the wind is blowing. If it blows from the north, it will be clear and cool. From the south, there will be more rain. From the east, expect storms and from the west clearing skies and slightly warmer temperatures.

Mid-level or medium clouds are divided into:

- Nimbostratus: thick, dark skies with low clouds that have persistent and sometimes heavy rain for long periods of time
- Altostratus: sun is visible through a hazy veil, white or grey uniform cloud. Periods of continuous rain or even snow on the way.
- Altocumulus: the famous, rippled "mackerel sky" which provides a brilliant display early mornings or evenings. Cold weather is on the way in winter, and in summer expect thunderstorms.

High clouds are divided into:

- Cirrostratus: Thin layer of cloud, sometimes hiding sun or moon, and often producing a "halo" effect. When these thicken a warm front is approaching. When the halo effect is this high in the sky, no rain on the way.
- Cirrocumulus: Small, wispy white clouds that indicate fair but cooler weather.
- Cirrus: Very white, very wispy clouds made of ice crystals that occur in fair weather, so no rain on the way.

Another trick which I use, as from my back garden I have a great view of all the air traffic passing along the East coast of England, is to watch the contrails left behind from the jets flying off to distant shores. If these trails dissipate quickly, it means that the air is dry, and usually will stay so for the near future. The longer these trails remain, the more moisture is in the air, which might indicate an approaching period of wet weather.

Here are some wonderful folk sayings to help predict the weather. Some of them are true, some of them not quite so much. Give them a try and see for yourself!

Red sky at night, sailors' delight.
Red sky in the morning, sailors take warning.

Flies will swarm before a storm.

When smoke descends, good weather ends. (Look out at chimneys for
this one in winter.)

Rain before seven, fine by eleven.

Snow like cotton, soon forgotten.
Snow like meal, it'll snow a good deal.

Frogs call to the coming rain
But in the sun are quiet again.

Part Four

Enchantment

Chapter Thirteen

Rites and Rituals

We previously looked at the word, enchantment (*en chantement*, "to sing into") as that which brings the songs of magic and the universe together so there is a flow, balance and harmony as well as a guiding, directive force. We can use enchantment in our lives for the same reason, to re-enchant our daily lives with the magical and the mystical, through the use of prayers and chants for mundane tasks, seasonal rites and celebrations as well as specially-performed magical workings.

Daily Prayers and Chants (re-weaving the connection of awen)

Awen, or inspiration, consists of the connecting threads that bind the universe together in relationship. When we awaken ourselves to this vast network of threads, we see that each one is important, and that the boundaries between what is sacred and what is mundane become blurred, as every action that we take has meaning, in this world and in the Otherworld. We can use daily prayers and chants to help us reweave this connection, or we can simply pay more attention to what it is that we are doing. For instance, we get up in the morning, and we go to the loo. We get dressed, then feed the cats, clean the litter boxes, make the coffee and have a smoothie. We then get to work. Where is the connection here, in a magical, mystical sense? How can we see the threads that bind us together in these everyday mundane tasks?

It really does require discipline, attention and practice. Let's take the example of getting up in the morning and really *pay attention*. As soon as we open our eyes, we can take a deep breath, and bring ourselves back into our bodies once again. *Inhabit your body fully.* This is the key to living in the moment, to being integrated, to feeling the threads of awen, of inspiration. So often we inhabit our minds, but not our bodies. Let's change this now.

Fully feeling inside your body, connect with your ancestors. You haven't even got out of bed yet. You are still breathing, feeling your body, the songs of your ancestors flowing through your blood. They are always with you. Give thanks to your ancestors. Meister Eckhart said that if the only prayer one ever says is thank you that is sufficient. Gratitude is one of the greatest gifts we can give to the world, including ourselves.

Mindfully, you sit up, placing your feet upon the floor. Take a moment to really feel the floor under you. Feel the solidity of the house, and stand up. Give thanks that you have a roof over your head, and a place of safety. Go to the loo, (and give thanks for indoor plumbing, especially in winter!) and dress for the day. Go to a window. Look out, and see what is happening in your landscape. Watch the sun rise, if you can, or look out into the inky blackness of a British morning in winter. If you are able, go outside and take few deep breaths. If not, open a window for a moment to feel the air on your skin, smelling the scents of the season. Give thanks to the ancestors of place, those who have gone before and who now provide you with life. They are the soil upon which you walk, the materials with which your house was built. Look at any flora and fauna around you, and give thanks to all that share this landscape with you.

Then go and light a candle and some incense, and offer your practice up to those who guide you. It could be a god, as well as ancestors of tradition. Give thanks for all that they have taught you, and for all that you still have to learn. Give thanks for being able to receive the wisdom. Give thanks that they are a part of your life. Take a few minutes to connect with deity, if you wish. Remember, it's all about relationship. Allow deity to flood your soul, and allow your soul to flood deity in return. You can either leave the candle and incense burning, or put it out to light tomorrow. Be sensible.

Then go and feed the cats, make the coffee. In feeding the cats, honour their souls and their presence in your life. Be grateful for them. As the coffee machine trickles water through the ground beans, give thanks for clean drinking water, for the farmers who grew the crop. As you make your smoothie, really look and honour each ingredient that you put in, thinking about where it came from, what land, what brought it to your kitchen countertop. Give thanks that you have food to eat, and a home to eat it in. When eating, you can say a short prayer beforehand, of gratitude and thanks.

You can continue this throughout the day. Reweaving the connection can be a wonderful exercise in seeing just how imaginative you can be in giving thanks to all that you have. It is also a wonderful lesson in just how much we in the Western world have to be thankful for. Though we are bombarded by horror and negativity each and every day through the media, we can remember the small things that bring us joy. We can be kind, and we can search for kindness in others. We can remember even though there may lie some very dark days before us, with the world's powers seemingly going berserk, that even the smallest person can make a difference. Remember that there are good people out there, working hard to give homeless people a better life. Remember that there are people giving first-aid and risking their own lives in war-torn counties and cities. Remember that the oak tree outside your window is providing you with oxygen. Remember your loved ones who support you, your children who carry you in their very being. Awake, and aware, we become attuned to the flow of the earth's energies, of the land, the sea and sky. And we are grateful.

- What are some things we can do, right here, right now, to reweave that connection?
- What can we do as soon as we get home, to reweave that connection?
- What can we do before we go to bed?
- What can we do at work?

• What can we do at play?

Through nurturing the connection and reweaving the threads, we are nurturing our own souls. We are truly seeing our place in the web of existence. We desperately need that nourishment. Too often we think that humans are simply messing everything up, but we have to acknowledge that even though it seems the majority of people might be doing so, there are a good number of people working towards the exact opposite, ourselves included. In the darkness of winter, it's easy to lose our way. Not guided by a great amount of light here in the UK, we can easily slip into darkness and depression. But we must remember that the spark of awen lies in each and every one of us. We have to seek out that spark in ourselves, and then we can see it reflected in the world. If we are attuned to the awen within, to the inspiration of connection, then we can weave those threads in everything that we do. Then, our path is guided by the brilliant, shining threads of existence.

Daily Prayers

Here are some examples of daily prayers that I use to help re-weave the connection. As a devotee of Brighid, I pray to Her every day, but you can change the wording to any deity you work with.

A Prayer Upon Rising

I kindle my soul at the hearthfire of Brighid.
Flame of courage, flame of joy, drops of awen be upon my lips, my work.
May Brighid guide me in all my endeavours, this day and every day.
May the light of illumination be upon me, may the blessings of Brighid flow through me.
May her fiery arrow bring forth awen, to shine upon all kith and kin.

A Daily Prayer and Meditation (to be performed at your altar each morning)

In Brighid's name I light the flame.
Come into the sacred waters, lady of the three strong fires:
in the cauldron, in the belly, in the head: Brighid.
Lady of the sacred flame,
lady of the holy well,
lady of poetry, smithcraft and healing,
white serpent energy of Albion,
I honour you for all that you are with all that I am.

A Blessing Prayer for the Home (to be performed each morning and/or just before bed)

A blessing be upon this hearth and this home,
and all who dwell within.
A blessing be upon my Lady,
a blessing be upon this land.
May there be peace in our hearts and minds, and towards all fellow
beings.
May we be the awen.

A Prayer before Meals

I give my thanks for this food that I am about to eat.
May it lend health, strength and nourishment to me.
I give my thanks to the spirits of land, sea and sky.
I honour all the times, and all the tides.

A Sunset Prayer (I prefer to sing this as the sun sets)

Hail fair sun the day is done.
We take the rest that we have won.
Your shining light guides our way.
Blessed thanks for this day.

A Prayer Just Before Sleep

I rest my soul in the arms of Brighid.
Lady of peace, lady of healing;
blessings of the sacred flame be upon me.
Protecting flame, the light in the darkness.
May her waters soothe my soul.
Lady, watch over me as I sleep, this night and every night.
May my love for you guide me in all that I do.
May we be the awen.

Have a look at the *Carmina Gadelica*, a tome previously mentioned that captures much wisdom and folklore from previous centuries. In it you will find charms and chants for everything, from harvesting herbs to churning the butter. You can be inspired by this work, to create your own charms and chants in order to bring more magic into your everyday life. Also look up superstitions and folklore from your area, such as the correct way to hang a horseshoe, or what to do when you come upon a "fairy ring". There are lots of sayings (and doings) for example, which can be fun to incorporate into your daily life, such as:

- If you find a holey (holed) stone on the beach, look through hole and you will see the spirits of the sea
- You can also hang a holey stone in the stable, to stop the horses from being "fairy ridden" at night (this is when your horse is unwell in the morning; obviously take good care of the animal and call the vet too!)
- After eating a boiled chicken egg, punch a hole in the bottom of the shell to stop evil witches from going to sea and sinking ships
- Make a wish when you see the first robin of winter
- Doff your cap, salute or greet any magpie you see

You can also learn some country crafts, such as making your own hand-dipped candles, brewing your own beer, cider or wine, or growing your own herbs. You can learn how to pickle fruits and vegetables, how to make jam or your own yoghurt. Research family recipes and honour your ancestors with any skill and talent that you may have in the kitchen. You can also tend a local area and keep it clean, clear and honoured. If you're lucky enough to live near a well, you can reinstate the ancient art of well-dressing with each festival of the year. All of these and more are various ways in which the Craft of the Hedge Druid comes alive each and every day.

Rites and Rituals

In working with the Hedge Druid's Craft, we have knowledge of the rites and rituals from both Wicca and Druidry. We can incorporate this into our Craft, to cast circles and use the ritual tools that we wish to include in our tradition as we walk our own path. It is beyond the scope of this introductory work to discuss fully all aspects of Wiccan and Druid ritual, but for more information please see the Bibliography and Further Reading at the end of this book, where you will find all you need to know about such things as circle casting, invocation and more in both traditions. For a detailed guide on the Druid tradition, there is my book *The Crane Bag: A Druid's Guide to Ritual Tools and Practices* that will complement the Hedge Druid's Craft nicely.

Here are some ideas for rites and rituals which you can perform at each of the eight festivals in the Wheel of the Year. Always leave an offering for the Fair Folk at the end of each working, to give back for all that we have received, in true honourable relationship.

Samhain

As this is the time when the veils between the worlds are thin, the Hedge Druid's Craft concerns working with the ancestors and the Fair Folk at this time of the year. She can travel to the Lowerworld to contact her ancestral spirit guide, or her fey spirit guide in order to glean information on the work that she should strive towards in the coming year. As Samhain marks the end of the old year and the beginning of the new, this is a perfect time to make "resolutions", and dream them up during the long winter months in the ways that you can make a change in your world for the better.

A rite for Samhain might be:

Take an apple and cut it in half through the middle of the fruit, not down the stem. When you open the apple into two halves, you should see a five-pointed star in the middle. The Celtic colours of red and white, the colours of the Otherworld, lie before you, and the energy of earth, air, fire, water and spirit. At your liminal working place, you can make an offering of one half of the apple to those who you work with in the Otherworld, and retain the other half for yourself to remind and connect you to the Otherworld. If you can, plant one of the seeds to keep near you, and nourish the tree of the Otherworld. Apple trees have long had associations with the Otherworld, being the trees that grew on Avalon, the Isle of Apples. Many myths and folklore contain stories of apples and enchantment, and so this is the perfect tool for walking between the worlds at this time of year, when the last of the apples are being harvested.

Winter Solstice

As this is the time of the longest night, holding an all-night vigil is a great way to attune yourself to the energy of darkness and rest, of winter and the earth. And when the sun rises in the morning, allow its light to wash over and inspire you. The Druids performed a ritual called *imbas forosna*, where a person was moved from utter darkness and sensory deprivation to bright light. To perform imbas forosna, find a place where you can eliminate all sources of light, if possible. A room indoors is probably the safest place, where you can draw the curtains and blinds. A cave out in the wilds is ideal, but of course all safety precautions must be taken first. You don't want to be sharing this space with anyone/anything else! If you can't achieve utter darkness either indoors or out, then take a cloak or a blindfold with you. You can wrap yourself in the cloak, or lay it over you to shield out all light, or simply place the blindfold over your eyes.

You can do this in a ritual circle, which would be the best place for such workings. Feel free to say prayers beforehand, drum or meditate. Then simply lie down and spend time in the darkness, allowing your thoughts to slow down over time. If you fall asleep, do not worry, for this too is a powerful form of work. When you wake, tell yourself the story of what you have just dreamed so that you will remember it. Then, after a few hours or at dawn, whether you have stayed awake or just woken up, throw off the cloak, tear off the blindfold, open the curtains and roll up the blind, immersing yourself in the light of day, moving from darkness to light. See what impressions, thoughts, feelings and emotions strike you as you move suddenly into the light. After you have undergone this experience, journal it right away so that you won't forget any of it.

Imbolc

Imbolc is a gentle festival, where we honour the first signs of spring after a long winter. It has long been dedicated to the goddess Brighid who has associations with fire and water. Allow this time of year to fill your soul, the air still cold but the warmth of the light from the strengthening sun inspiring you to go out into the worlds (this world and the Otherworld) and do the work that you have to do. You can light a candle to dedicate yourself at this time to your work, having spent the winter months thinking long and deeply about it. Now is the time to state your intention clearly. You can carve words or symbols into the candle that represent your work, and strew herbs around it to lend their energies (see A Basic Candle Spell in the next section). As you light the candle, state your intention clearly, calling upon the ancestors and the Fair

Folk, the gods and goddesses to bear witness. This is not an oath to be made lightly. Meditate upon the candle's flame for as long as you wish. Then take a bowl of spring water and anoint yourself with it. I like to collect water from Chalice Well and the White Spring in Glastonbury every time I visit, and I use this special, holy water for use in rituals and in spellcraft. You can draw the shape of a crescent moon upon your brow with the water, or place any other symbols which have meaning to you upon your body. It is also a good time for healing work, and anointing yourself with sacred water on areas of your body that need healing can kick-start the process (as well as following good medical and spiritual advice).

Spring Equinox

A wonderful liminal time, when day and night are equal, the Spring Equinox is a good time for spellwork that requires turning the tides and affecting change in the world. If performed at special liminal places such as the seashore, or a forest edge, or in a hedgerow, it can add extra power to the work. This is a good time of year to physically begin the work that you dreamt over the long winter months and dedicated yourself to during Imbolc. At this time of year, fields and tools such as ploughs were often blessed and "charmed", and so you can also do this with your ritual tools. Begin your spellcrafting to bring about the change that you want to see in the world.

Spellcraft is not enough, however, for we must also physically and mentally work to create the change that we want to see in the world. So, dependent upon your intention and dedication, now you must physically and mentally do the work too that you have set yourself upon. It's not enough to just think about doing something; one must do it. The Hedge Druid's Craft is about helping yourself, as well as others. It's about what you do in the world, first and foremost, not what you think.

Beltane

This is another traditional time when the veils between the worlds are thin, and we can encounter beings from the Otherworld easily as we slip between the worlds. It is traditionally a time to honour the Fair Folk, as well as the fertility of the land in hopes of great abundance in the autumn. We can work with the Fair Folk to ensure that our endeavours are successful.

In your liminal place, call to the Fair Folk, to allow you to communicate with all those who are in tune with your intention. Your Lowerworld guides may appear, as well as others who can impart wisdom and information on the work that you are doing. It is a good time to allow the awen, the inspiration to flow and to open yourself to new possibilities. The flowers of hawthorn (a known Faery Tree) are out, and you can take a sprig and wear it upon your person (with the tree's and the Fair Folk's permission first) as you weave your magic in the world. Be open, but also beware. You must decide for yourself what information you will use, and whether it is for the benefit of the whole. Not all of the Fair Folk have your best interests at heart, for they are creatures of nature with their own agenda. This is a good time of year to communicate with them and learn more of their work, how you can help them and vice versa to bring about harmony in all the worlds. Ask them what they would like to see happen in your world, and tell them likewise what you would like to achieve. You might just find the Fair Folk comply.

Summer Solstice

The time of the greatest light, this is a good time of the year to harness the energy towards your goals. Riding the tide, we can stand in the heat of the noon-day sun and allow its energy to flow through us, empowering our bodies, souls and our work. We might use herbs traditional to this time of year, such as St John's Wort, to further boost our work. Know, though, that after this special time we begin the descent back into the dark half of the year, and so we also work with the turning tide.

A good place to perform magic at this time of year is at the seashore, when the tide is moving from high tide to low tide. Stand at the water's edge at high tide, and cast any spells to aid you in the work that you have committed yourself to for your local environment and community. Use the time of the highest tide and then, when it begins to recede, sit back and watch as the water takes the spell and returns it to the realms of the Otherworld beneath the sea (a very Celtic motif). Allow the work to move from you and out into the world. (See A Basic Sea Spell at the end of this chapter for more information.)

Lughnasadh

This is the time of the first harvest, when the wheat that has ripened in the summer months is ready for harvest, turning golden as the sun. This is also when, hopefully, we begin to see the results of the work that we have done throughout the year. Know, however, that there is still much work to be done, and we cannot rest on our laurels!

If you can, visit a field of wheat and pluck a few sheaves that have escaped the field boundary. You will often find some growing on the verge next to a bridleway near a farmer's field. Take these home and soak them in water to make them pliable. You can then plait them, weaving together your intention for the rest of the harvest season. There are many different ways of making "corn dollies"; do some research and see what you are able to achieve in this traditional country craft. You can keep the corn dolly until Samhain, when it can then be burned on the fire as the harvest is over and we must dream and scheme up new things for the coming year, or re-hash a plan that didn't work and try again, gazing in to the fire as the dolly burns for insights as to how to proceed differently this time around.

Autumn Equinox

Another liminal time, where darkness and light are equal, this is the perfect opportunity to take stock of what you have harvested from your efforts, and what still needs to be achieved before Samhain and the coming of winter. After this, you will need to let go, even as the autumn leaves fall from the trees. Go to a deciduous tree, and watch as its leaves change colour. Know that this is the winding down of the year, and that your life is reflected in the season. You have worked hard, and now the magic appears even as the bright colours of autumn turn the woodland into golden and fiery hues, reflecting and honouring the last of the bright sunshine of the warmer days. Keep a vigil on a tree, and weave a spell of release into a specific leaf, something which you need to let go of in order to move forward. Return to that tree every day and note when that specific leaf has fallen. The magic has been set in motion. Now you must let go as the tree has let go of the leaf, to allow the past to fall away, to nourish you and inform you even as you dream it all up again.

Chapter Fourteen

Spells and Charms

A Basic Candle Spell

Take a candle of an appropriate colour to use in your work. As a very basic guide, red is for love and passion, pink for emotions, blue for healing, green for the environment, brown for animals, yellow for inspiration, purple for magical strength, black for release of negativity. White candles are used for purification, and they can be used to replace any other colour that you may not be able to obtain. Alternatively, you can always use wax crayons to decorate or colour your candle as you see fit!

Sit with your candle and meditate upon the work that you wish to achieve. Then, stating your intention clearly, pour your energy into the candle. Allow energy to flow from your hands into the candle. When you have poured enough into the candle, you can then add more strength to it by carving words or symbols into it, still holding your intention. Then, place the candle in a holder and light it with a match. As you strike the match, keep your intention in your mind, and as you bring the match to the candle's wick, visualise the power of fire igniting your work. Sit before the candle and meditate upon the flame, still holding the visualisation of the end result of your spellwork coming to fruition. You can add herbs around the base of the candle, if you so wish, to allow them to add their magical energy to your work. You can infuse the herbs with your intention and energy in exactly the same way as you did the candle. See with your mind's eye a cone of power rising from the herbs around the candle, blending with the candle's flame and sending the power out into the world.

A Basic Sea Spell

Go to the water at the proper time for your spellwork. You might be working with a low tide, or a high tide, or that point where one tide turns to the next. Be sure to check tide timetables, and be safe; don't get stranded somewhere when the water begins to come back in. Take some herbs with you, and infuse them with your energy and intention. At the time of the highest or lowest tide you can throw the herbs into the water and allow the energy of the water to influence the outcome upon contact, or to honour the season and time of the year (such as the Summer Solstice rite). Working with the moon as well as the tides doubly empowers your work, as the moon controls the tides.

Some herbs for simple sea spells might be:

Vervain: – a good all around herb for all magical uses
St John's Wort: – prosperity, healing and magical strength, Summer Solstice
Juniper: – –protection and purification
Rowan: – working with the Fair Folk
Thyme: – purification, contacting the Otherworld and Ancestors
Heather: – for good luck, protection and to induce rain
Dandelion: – opening psychic awareness, strength and Summer Solstice
Mugwort: – second sight, contacting Fair Folk, Summer Solstice

A Basic Spell/Chant/Charm

Here is an example of the basic wording for a spell, chant or charm which you can use in your work. To be used at your special liminal place, at an altar or wherever you wish to work, and can be used in conjunction with the above two basic spells and for all spell-crafting.

Power of sun and moon be here
Power of wind and rain
Power of land, sea and sky
Splendour of fire, speed of lightning

Swiftness of wind
Depth of sea
Firmness of rock
Aid me in my work
The awen I sing
From the deep I bring it
The awen I sing
A connected river which flows
I know its might
I know its flow
Awen, awen, awen

By the power of three times three
This is my will, so may it be.

Conclusion

This work is but an introduction into the Hedge Druid's Craft. There are countless spells, associations, tools, practices, folklore and wisdom to be used in the work. We must remember that everything we do affects the whole, as we are all part of an interconnected web of existence. The threads of existence shimmer with awen in deep, honourable, sustainable relationship. It is to these threads that we train when we work with the Hedge Druid's Craft, to work for the benefit of the whole, fully understanding our place in the environment and as part of an ecosystem. We walk between the worlds, bringing back knowledge, wisdom and healing for ourselves and our communities.

I hope that these words have enchanted you and inspired you in your work. May we be the awen.

Bibliography and Further Reading

Beth, R. (2008) *The Green Hedge Witch*, Robert Hale

Beth, R. (2001) *The Hedge Witch's Way*, Robert Hale

Carmichael, A. (1992) *Carmina Gadelica: Hymns and Incantations*, Floris Books

Cunningham, S. (2004) *Cunningham's Encyclopedia of Wicca in the Kitchen*, Llewellyn

Cunninhgam, S. (1993) *Earth, Air, Fire & Water: More Techniques of Natural Magic*, Llewellyn

Cunningham, S. (1984) *Earth Power: Techniques of Natural Magic*, Llewellyn

Cunningham, S. (1993) *Living Wicca: A Further Guide for the Solitary Practitioner*, Llewellyn

Cunningham, S. (1988) *Wicca: A Guide for the Solitary Practitioner*, Llewellyn

Cunningham et Harrington (2003) *The Magical Household: Spells and Rituals for the Home*, Llewellyn

Cunningham et Harrington (2005), *Spell Crafts: Creating Magical Objects*, Llewellyn

Daimler, M. (2011) *By Land, Sea and Sky: A Selection of Paganized Prayers and Charms from Volumes 1 & 2 of the Carmina Gadelica*, Lulu

Draco, Melusine (2016) *The Secret People: Parish-Pump Witchcraft, Wise-Women and Cunning Ways*, Moon Books

Draco, Melusine (2012) *Traditional Witchcraft for Fields and Hedgerows*, John Hunt Publishing

Forest, D. (2013) *The Druid Shaman: Exploring the Celtic Otherworld*, Moon Books

Freeman, M. (2000) *Kindling the Celtic Spirit*, Harper Collins

Gooley, T. (2011) *The Natural Navigator Pocket Guide*, Virgin Books

Green, M. (1995) *A Witch Alone: Thirteen Moons to Master Natural Magic*, Thorsons

Hopman, E. E. (1995) *A Druid's Herbal for the Sacred Earth Year*, Inner Traditions Bear and Company

Hopman, E. E. (2008) *A Druid's Herbal of Sacred Tree Medicine*, Inner Traditions International

Hughes, K. (2016) *The Book of Celtic Magic: Transformative Teachings from the Cauldron of Awen*, Llewellyn

Hutton, R. (2011) *Blood and Mistletoe: The History of the Druids in Britain*, Yale University Press

Hutton, R. (2001) *The Triumph of the Moon: A History of Modern Pagan Witchcraft*, Oxford University Press

Jenner et Smith, (2008) *The Outdoor Pocket Bible: Every Outdoor Rule of Thumb at Your Fingertips*, Crimson Publishing

Kynes, S. (2015) *Star Magic: The Wisdom of the Constellations for Pagan and Wiccans*, Llewellyn

Matthews, C. & Matthews, J. (1994) *Encyclopaedia of Celtic Wisdom: A Celtic Shaman's Sourcebook*, Element

Matthews, J. (2001) *The Celtic Shaman: A Practical Guide*, Rider

McGarry, G. (2007) *Brighid's Healing: Ireland's Celtic Medicine Traditions*, Green Magic

Restall Orr, E. (2004) *Living Druidry: Magical Spirituality for the Wild Soul*, London, Piatkus Books Ltd

Restall Orr, E. (1998) *Principles of Druidry*, Thorsons

Restall Orr, E. (2000) *Ritual: A Guide to Life, Love and Inspiration*, Thorsons

Restall Orr, E. (2014) *Druid Priestess: An Intimate Journey Through the Pagan Year*, Thorsons

Seal, J. (2008) *Hedgerow Medicine: Harvest and Make Your Own Herbal Remedies*, Merlin Unwin Books

Seal et Seal (2014) *The Herbalist's Bible: John Parkinson's Lost Classic Rediscovered*, Merlin Unwin Books

Starhawk, (1989) *The Spiral Dance: A Rebirth of the Ancient Religion of the Great Goddess*, Harper One

Struthers, J. (2009) *Red Sky at Night: The Book of Lost Countryside Wisdom*, Ebury Press

Sutton et Mann, (2013) *Druid Magic: The Practice of Celtic Wisdom*, Llewellyn

Toulson, S. (1981) *East Anglia: Walking the Ley Lines and Ancient Tracks*, Wildwood House Limited

van der Hoeven, J. (2014) *The Awen Alone: Walking the Path of the Solitary Druid*, Moon Books

van der Hoeven, J. (2017) *The Crane Bag: A Druid's Guide to Ritual Tools and Practices*, Moon Books

van der Hoeven, J. (2014) *Dancing with Nemetona: A Druid's Exploration of Sanctuary and Sacred Space*, Moon Books

Other books by the author

The Awen Alone: Walking the Path of the Solitary Druid
Druidry is a wonderful, spiritually fulfilling life path. Through the
magic of Druidry, we build deep and abiding relationships with
the natural world around us, and through our connection to the
natural environment we walk a path of truth, honour and service.
Throughout the ages, people have withdrawn from the world in
order to connect more fully with it. This book is an introductory
guide for those who wish to walk the Druid path alone, for
however long a time. It is about exploration and connection with
the natural world, and finding our place within it. It covers the
basics of Druidry and how, when applied to everyday life, enriches
it with a sense of beauty, magic and mystery. This book is for those
people who feel called to seek their own path, to use their wit and
intelligence, compassion and honour to create their own tradition
within Druidry.

The Crane Bag: A Druid's Guide to Ritual Tools and Practices
An introduction to the ritual tools and practices found in the Druid
tradition. Held deeply within Celtic mythology, the crane bag is
both a symbol of sovereignty, as well as an item containing the
ritual tools of the Druid. With the proper use, it can further the
Druid in working with the tides of nature, finding his or her own
place in the environment, living in balance, harmony and peace.
In ritual, these tools and practices can guide one to deeper levels
of meaning and understanding within the tradition, helping the
Druid on his or her journey through life and towards integration
with the natural world.

Zen Druidry: Living a Natural Life with Full Awareness
Taking both Zen and Druidry and integrating them into your life
can be a wonderful and ongoing process of discovery, not only of

the self but of the entire world around you. Looking at ourselves and at the natural world around us, we realise that everything is in constant flux: like waves on the ocean, they are all united as a body of water. Even after the wave crashes upon the shore, the ocean is still there, the wave is still there; it has merely changed its form. The aim of this text is an introduction to how Zen teachings and Druidry can combine, creating a peaceful life path that is completely and utterly dedicated to the here and now, to the earth and her rhythms, and to the flow that is life itself.

Dancing With Nemetona: A Druid's Exploration of Sanctuary and Sacred Space

Nemetona is an ancient goddess whose song is heard deep within the earth and also deep within the human soul. She is the Lady of Sanctuary, of Sacred Groves and Sacred Spaces. She is present within the home, within our sacred groves, our rites and in all the spaces which we hold dear to our hearts. She also lies within, allowing us to feel at ease wherever we are in the world through her energy of holding and of transformation. She is the energy of sacred space, where we can stretch out our souls and truly come alive, filled with the magic of potential. Rediscover this ancient goddess and dance with a Druid to the songs of Nemetona. Learn how to reconnect with this goddess in ritual, songs, chants, meditation and more.

Zen for Druids: A Further Guide to Integration, Compassion and Harmony with Nature

The teachings of Zen Buddhism combined with the earth-based tradition of Druidry can create a holistic way of life that is deeply integrated with the seasons, the environment and the present moment. In soul-deep relationship we can use the techniques and wisdom from both traditions to find balance and harmony within our own lives. In this follow-up work to the Pagan Portals Zen Druidry by the same author, we explore the concepts of the Dharma (the Buddha's teachings) and how they relate to the wisdom of the Druid tradition. We also look at the Wheel of the Year in modern Druidry with regards to the Dharma, incorporating the teachings into every seasonal festival in an all-encompassing celebration of nature. We explore meditation, mindfulness, animism and integration with nature, learning how to find sustainable relationship in the work which we do, opening our souls to the here and now and seeing the beauty and wonder that enchants our lives in every waking moment. Step into a new life, fully awake and aware to the beauty of the natural world.

The Stillness Within: Finding Inner Peace in a Conflicted World

A collection of writings on finding inner peace, based on Zen principles, meditation and more. It explores aspects of Zen meditation, compassion and learning how to live in a more peaceful state of being. It consists of small, bite-size chapters that are easily understood and can be picked up whenever a little inspiration is needed. We can be at peace even in a world that seems to be going to pieces. We can be at peace when others are trying to cut us down. We can be at peace in a world that is so materialistic and consumer-driven that it is making itself extinct. That peace is the core of our being. That peace is within each and every one of us, if we are willing to see it. Through the opening of the eyes and the soul, we find that still, deep pool of being and of knowing, and there we reign supreme. We find the stillness within.

Honour-bound: She Must Win Back her Life, and Her Soul
(Fantasy Fiction)

Honour. Faedriel Falconwing, having grown up in the dark city streets of Loviath Citadel, has known no such thing. Then one day events happen to make her question her way of life and all that she has known. Taken as a child from her elven father, Faedriel was raised by her human mother in the Thieves and Assassins' Guild.

She rose within the ranks of the Guild until one day she is called to kill a priest of the Goddess Morritria, Lady of the Forest. Before she completes her mission, the priest gives her a strange message from the goddess: that she is called to regain her lost honour, and save her soul. Faedriel flees the Citadel and begins the quest to reclaim her elven heritage and her honour. Pursued by the Guild for desertion she finds danger, excitement and love as she tries to win back her soul.

About the author

Joanna van der Hoeven was born in Quebec, Canada. She moved to the UK in 1998, where she now lives with her husband in a small village in Suffolk, near the coast of the North Sea.

Joanna is a Druid, author, teacher, poet, singer and dancer. She has studied with Emma Restall Orr and the Order of Bards, Ovates and Druids. She has a BA Hons English Language and Literature degree. She is currently the Media Co-Ordinator for The Druid Network. She is also co-founder and tutor at Druid College UK. She gives talks and workshops regularly on meditation, Druidry, Zen Buddhism and more.

For more information, please visit
www.joannavanderhoeven.com

We think you will also enjoy...

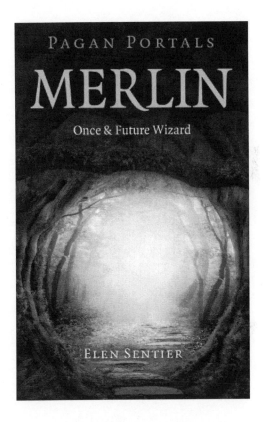

Merlin: Once and Future Wizard, Elen Sentier
Merlin in history, Merlin in mythology, Merlin through the ages and his
continuing relevance

*...a grand and imaginative work that introduces the reader to the many
faces of the mysterious Merlin.*
Morgan Daimler

978-1-78535-453-3 (paperback)
978-1-78535-454-0 (e-book)

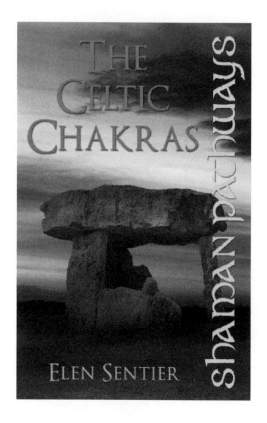

Celtic Chakras, Elen Sentier

Tread the British native shaman's path, explore the Goddess
hidden in the ancient stories; walk the Celtic chakra spiral
labyrinth.

*Rich with personal vision, the book is an interesting exploration of
wholeness*
Emma Restall Orr

978-1-78099-506-9 (paperback)
978-1-78099-507-6 (e-book)

Druid Shaman, Danu Forest

A practical guide to Celtic shamanism with exercises and
techniques as well as traditional lore for exploring the Celtic
Otherworld

A sound, practical introduction to a complex and wide-ranging subject
Philip Shallcrass

978-1-78099-615-8 (paperback)
978-1-78099-616-5 (e-book)

Kitchen Witchcraft, Rachel Patterson
Take a glimpse at the workings of a Kitchen Witch and share in
the crafts

*A wonderful little book which will get anyone started on Kitchen
Witchery. Informative, and easy to follow*
Janet Farrar & Gavin Bone

978-1-78099-843-5 (paperback)
978-1-78099-842-8 (e-book)

Moon Magic, Rachel Patterson

An introduction to working with the phases of the Moon

...a delightful treasury of lore and spiritual musings that should be essential to any planetary magic-worker's reading list.

David Salisbury

978-1-78279-281-9 (paperback)
978-1-78279-282-6 (e-book)

Best Selling Pagan Portals & Shaman Pathways

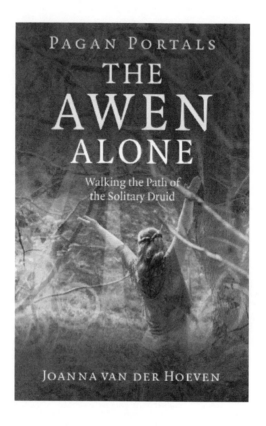

The Awen Alone, Joanna van der Hoeven
An introductory guide for the solitary Druid

Joanna's voice carries the impact and knowledge of the ancestors,
combined with the wisdom of contemporary understanding.
Cat Treadwell

978-1-78279-547-6 (paperback)
978-1-78279-546-9 (e-book)

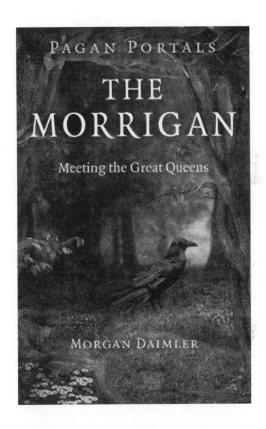

The Morrigan, Morgan Daimler

On shadowed wings and in raven's call, meet the ancient Irish
Goddess of war, battle, prophecy, death, sovereignty, and magic

*…a well-researched and heartfelt guide to the Morrigan from a fellow
devotee and priestess*
Stephanie Woodfield

978-1-78279-833-0 (paperback)
978-1-78279-834-7 (e-book)

Moon Books

PAGANISM & SHAMANISM

What is Paganism? A religion, a spirituality, an alternative belief system, nature worship? You can find support for all these definitions (and many more) in dictionaries, encyclopaedias, and text books of religion, but subscribe to any one and the truth will evade you. Above all Paganism is a creative pursuit, an encounter with reality, an exploration of meaning and an expression of the soul. Druids, Heathens, Wiccans and others, all contribute their insights and literary riches to the Pagan tradition. Moon Books invites you to begin or to deepen your own encounter, right here, right now.

If you have enjoyed this book, why not tell other readers by posting a review on your preferred book site.

Recent bestsellers from Moon Books are:

Journey to the Dark Goddess
How to Return to Your Soul
Jane Meredith
Discover the powerful secrets of the Dark Goddess and
transform your depression, grief and pain into healing
and integration.
Paperback: 978-1-84694-677-6 ebook: 978-1-78099-223-5

Shamanic Reiki
Expanded Ways of Working with Universal Life Force Energy
Llyn Roberts, Robert Levy
Shamanism and Reiki are each powerful ways of healing; together,
their power multiplies. *Shamanic Reiki* introduces techniques to
help healers and Reiki practitioners tap ancient healing wisdom.
Paperback: 978-1-84694-037-8 ebook: 978-1-84694-650-9

Pagan Portals – The Awen Alone
Walking the Path of the Solitary Druid
Joanna van der Hoeven
An introductory guide for the solitary Druid, *The Awen Alone* will
accompany you as you explore, and seek out your own place
within the natural world.
Paperback: 978-1-78279-547-6 ebook: 978-1-78279-546-9

A Kitchen Witch's World of Magical Herbs & Plants
Rachel Patterson
A journey into the magical world of herbs and plants, filled with
magical uses, folklore, history and practical magic. By popular
writer, blogger and kitchen witch, Tansy Firedragon.
Paperback: 978-1-78279-621-3 ebook: 978-1-78279-620-6

Medicine for the Soul
The Complete Book of Shamanic Healing
Ross Heaven
All you will ever need to know about shamanic healing and how to
become your own shaman...
Paperback: 978-1-78099-419-2 ebook: 978-1-78099-420-8

Shaman Pathways – The Druid Shaman
Exploring the Celtic Otherworld
Danu Forest
A practical guide to Celtic shamanism with exercises and
techniques as well as traditional lore for exploring the Celtic
Otherworld.
Paperback: 978-1-78099-615-8 ebook: 978-1-78099-616-5

Traditional Witchcraft for the Woods and Forests
A Witch's Guide to the Woodland with Guided Meditations and
Pathworking
Melusine Draco
A Witch's guide to walking alone in the woods, with guided
meditations and pathworking.
Paperback: 978-1-84694-803-9 ebook: 978-1-84694-804-6

Wild Earth, Wild Soul
A Manual for an Ecstatic Culture
Bill Pfeiffer
Imagine a nature-based culture so alive and so connected,
spreading like wildfire. This book is the first flame...
Paperback: 978-1-78099-187-0 ebook: 978-1-78099-188-7

Naming the Goddess
Trevor Greenfield
Naming the Goddess is written by over eighty adherents and
scholars of Goddess and Goddess Spirituality.
Paperback: 978-1-78279-476-9 ebook: 978-1-78279-475-2

Shapeshifting into Higher Consciousness
Heal and Transform Yourself and Our World with Ancient
Shamanic and Modern Methods
Llyn Roberts
Ancient and modern methods that you can use every day to
transform yourself and make a positive difference in the world.
Paperback: 978-1-84694-843-5 ebook: 978-1-84694-844-2

Readers of ebooks can buy or view any of these bestsellers by
clicking on the live link in the title. Most titles are published in
paperback and as an ebook. Paperbacks are available in traditional
bookshops. Both print and ebook formats are available online.

Find more titles and sign up to our readers' newsletter at
http://www.johnhuntpublishing.com/paganism
Follow us on Facebook at
https://www.facebook.com/MoonBooks
and Twitter at https://twitter.com/MoonBooksJHP